## *STUDENT COMMENTS ON THE FITNESS OPTION PROGRAM*

"I will not hesitate to recommend this course to relatives, friends, and clients."

—RON MANN, CLINICAL PSYCHOLOGIST

"In nine years of education, this course was the richest and deepest I have encountered."

—MARK MORGENSTERN, PSYCHIATRIST

"There is a tremendous sense of inner quietness that springs from a few well-done exercises that seems not to be had elsewhere in our daily, chaotic lives. Sometimes the most challenging of exercises are those that seem the easiest—the deep relaxation and quieting of the mind."

—SHELLEY THOMPSON, VICE PRESIDENT OF COMMUNICATIONS

"An automobile accident twenty years ago left me with middle back, shoulder, and neck 'jamming.' Limited movement and constant pain were my reality. The exercises in the Fitness Option program have worked the miracle of release on my upper body. I experienced a limbering the first week and now, only a few months later, I have full range of motion and no pain. I will be forever grateful…."

—JEAN MUSCOTT, FUNERAL DIRECTOR

"Of all the courses I have taken in the last six years at the University of California, San Diego, this has been the most valuable. It has given a framework to my life."

—LINDA LUTZ, U.C.S.D. GRADUATE STUDENT

"I have found the techniques to be invaluable; I intend to practice them the rest of my life. I have a much better focus, am able to concentrate and relax better for longer periods of time, and have increased flexibility."

—MARSEE SKIDMORE, U.C.S.D. STUDENT

"I am a student at the University of California, San Diego and have two jobs and a family. The stress level is very high, but I am managing because of the skills gained in this course. I need less sleep, have fewer headaches and less muscle tension, and am less susceptible to daily pressures. Often I find myself stretching and breathing to calm myself."

—KAREN PICKENS, U.C.S.D. STUDENT

"The methods of breathing, deep relaxation, and slow, calm exercises are one of the most important aspects of my life. I am happier, healthier, and more nourishing and creative in personal relationships."

—SHARON WHITE, COMPUTER PROGRAMMER

"The tools of this course have made me very body aware and able to isolate tensions and release them as they start to occur. As an actor, the greatest benefit has been in helping me to overcome my problems with stage fright through the relaxation and breathing techniques."

—PETER COLLISON, DRAMATIST

Second Edition 1990
© 1988,1990 Valerie O'Hara

Cover design by Goss Keller Martinez, Inc.
Inside design by Michael Coombs, Clarity Design Guild
Photography by Allen F. Schmeltz, Christopher Kight Studios
Illustrations by Brent Spaulding

Published by La Jolla Institute for Stress Management
Nevada City, California

# THE
# FITNESS
## FIVE WEEKS TO HEALING STRESS
# OPTION

### BY
# VALERIE O'HARA, PH.D.

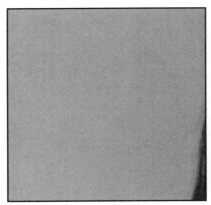

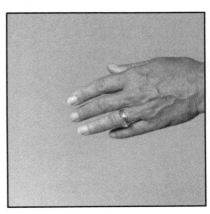
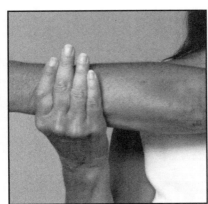
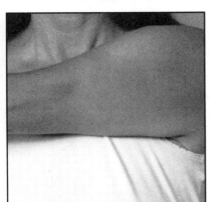

Pictured: Valerie O'Hara, author of *The Fitness Option*

# COMMENDATION

THIS EXTREMELY EFFECTIVE five-week strategy is an easy-to-follow and enjoyable approach to physical fitness, stress reduction, health, and well-being. I recommend this book to anyone who is interested in staying well or getting well. The book is a seminal contribution to the new field of Interactive Medicine—**a work of extraordinary merit.**

EDWARD A. TAUB, M.D.
Associate Professor at University of California, Irvine Medical School
President of Foundation For Health Awareness
Founder of Wellness Medicine
Author *Voyage to Wellness*
Author *Prescription for Life*
Medical Director, Center for Interactive Medicine, Tustin, California

# DEDICATION

TO MY HUSBAND, BRYAN, who has given me his support,
his love, and his patience.

TO DONALD AND ROSANNA WALTERS, for their inspiration and example.

"CHERISH YOUR VISIONS;

cherish your ideals;

cherish the music that stirs in your heart,

the beauty that forms in your mind,

the loveliness that drapes your purest thoughts,

for out of them will grow all delightful conditions,

all heavenly environments;

of these, if you but remain true to them,

your world will at last be built."

—JAMES ALLEN

# CONTENTS

**EACH WEEK INCLUDES:**  Lessson  ◆  Instant Stress Releaser
◆  Breathing Exercise  ◆  Weekly Routine  ◆  Detailed Instructions
on the Exercises  ◆  Deep Relaxation  ◆  Rewarding Yourself
◆  Weekly Review  ◆  Charting Your Progress

# ABOUT THE AUTHOR

I WILL SHARE WITH YOU how I came to write *The Fitness Option*. My love of movement began at an early age. I thoroughly enjoyed swinging and climbing on the jungle gym, and doing cartwheels across the lawn was a daily, exhilarating experience. At dawn, while the family slept, I often practiced handstands and headstands on my bed. Ballet, and later modern dance lessons, were a natural outgrowth of my love of being physically active.

At age seven my grandfather, an Olympic judge and referee, and author of a classic manual on ice skating, inspired me to 30 years of competition, show skating, and finally coaching in this graceful, creative sport. At 29 I was introduced to yoga. Yoga opened new directions in movement, adding the dimensions of breathing techniques and mental quiet to enhance exploration of the body. I found yoga also increased my flexibility in skating and helped me perform with less anxiety.

Drawing on years of training as an ice skater, intensive dance practice, two decades of experiencing many approaches to yoga, and intensives with physical therapists and flexibility conditioning instructors, I put together a five-week physical routine to increase flexibility and strength and release muscles tense due to stress.

The mental/emotional aspects of *The Fitness Option* are based on Western and Eastern psychotherapy and relaxation skills. Firstly, I journeyed beyond the physical aspects of yoga, discovering avenues to better understand both my mind and emotions. I learned skills to harmonize the conflicting cross currents within myself. Secondly, after thirteen years of self-exploration and teaching, I returned to graduate school in psychology and gained new perspectives on anxiety and stress and their effects on both the mind and the body. I gained practical experience in a two-year internship program for counseling and explored diverse approaches on how to optimize potential talent and happiness by reducing physical, mental, and emotional stress.

*The Fitness Option* is a result of my physical and mental training and experience in diverse fields. I have gathered together the specific benefits of each discipline to create a balanced, holistic approach to optimal health. *The Fitness Option* is unique in its detail, its eclectic information, and its safe format. It has been structured to help you learn and personalize the material easily. It is also designed for teachers to use in a class format.

On a personal note, I feel saddened when I find myself or others not taking care of the gift of life and health we have been given. Many of us suffer not from the trials and challenges of life but from our lack of a sense of self-worth and lack of self-care. In the 1990's we are at last beginning to reclaim and nurture the planet we have damaged. We need to make this same commitment to ourselves. This book is to aid you, the reader, in your journey of self-discovery and healing, a journey needed to live all the years of your life in well-being and happiness.

—VALERIE O'HARA
1990

# ACKNOWLEDGMENTS

AS A STUDENT, I want to thank and acknowledge the teachers who have taught me dance, ice skating, yoga, aerobics, swimming, and academics. I also appreciate the informal, valuable lessons gained from friends, acquaintances, and life itself. A special teacher of mine has said, "Happiness is in learning, not in teaching." This book is a product, in the largest sense, of all I have learned, and I am grateful.

Heartfelt thanks go to the many friends and relatives who encouraged me in the process of writing and put in long hours of reading and organizing the material presented here. These include Gale Baccaglini, Neil Murray, Lila Devi, Laura Hermann, Jane Simpson, Rachael Fleet, Holly McMillan, Joanne Myrup, Pamela Whitehouse, and Cathy Parojinog. Holly McMillan very generously loaned her laser printer in the final hours of organizing and printing. For the second edition, Derek Van Atta kindly loaned me the use of all of his computer equipment.

In this second edition of the book I owe special thanks to Ann Muldoon for her enthusiastic support, long hours of discussion, and creative suggestions. Michael Coombs gave untiringly of his expertise and enthusiasm during hours of consultation and creative design work. Debie Torkellson was there helping whenever I needed her with her fresh ideas, hours of design time, and friendship. Special thanks to Doctor Kent Baughman for his advice, knowledge, and discussions on the chapter *Stress and Your Lower Back*.

Special thanks go to my brother, Rob Whittemore, Professor Chris Norris, Dr. Edward Taub, Alan Heubert, and Carole Franz for their honest evaluations, red penciling, and excellent editing.

The book would not have been started nor have been finished without the tangible and intangible help of my husband, Bryan.

I will never forget Roland Burt of Macintosh Solutions in Del Mar, California, who retrieved the uncopied, nearly completed manuscript from the bowels of my computer, when every other computer expert had given up.

A special commendation is owed Allen Schmeltz for his excellent photography of Debie Torkellson, Bryan, and me doing the exercises, and to Brent Spaulding, who drew the illustrations.

I deeply thank Donald Walters for his example of giving unstintingly of himself, and sharing his wisdom, his caring, and his experience with all who cross his path.

I especially thank my father, Frank H. Whittemore, who has always been an inspiration to me through his quiet example of honesty, humility, generosity, and self-discipline. I appreciate his faith in me and his generous support in the publication of the first edition of *The Fitness Option*.

Heartfelt warmth goes to Jim Wagenschutz, Joy Furby, Cheryl Shaeffer, Arnell Ando, and Wil Perrine, for their support and generosity in the printing of this second edition of the book.

# PART I

# STRESS MANAGEMENT AND THE FITNESS OPTION

*We live as surface ripples on a lake, needing to re-discover the calm beneath, our core of inner quietude.*

# INTRODUCTION

# THE PROBLEM: STRESS

ONLY WHEN WE ARE IN HARMONY with ourselves physically and mentally can we experience the beauty within and around us and fully share with others. My life has been greatly enriched through learning how to relax at will both physically and mentally. Creative expression has blossomed with the removal of thwarting anxiety and physical pain. Each one of us can choose to live productive, energetic lives, based on an inner strength and calmness. Stress does not need to be a way of life.

For over ten years, though, stress has plagued our nation. According to the medical profession, 80-90% of today's illnesses are stress-related. Approaching life from a stress mode results in worry and anxiety that produce irritability, impatience, depression, and frustration. Such chronic expressions of stress open the flood gates to ulcers, migraine headaches, insomnia, backaches, diabetes, and cardiovascular diseases. They also result in corporate costs due to lost time and increased insurance rates.

### Author's Personal Experience of Stress

My own story illustrates the personal impact of stress. Surprisingly, I was not initially led to stress-reducing techniques and methods of healing because of poor health. For the last 21 years, I have been teaching stress management techniques, stretching, yoga, and meditation. I attribute my excellent health and youthful looks to my heredity, environment, and life-style.

Although I had been living and teaching techniques for a healthy, productive life, I was stunned by the results of letting go of my long-practiced relaxation skills. I only stopped to look at my mental and physical health after five years of intensive striving during which I had gradually stopped practicing the very skills I was teaching. On the credit side, at the end of five years I had completed my Ph.D. in counseling psychology, was licensed as a psychotherapist, had co-founded the La Jolla Institute For Stress Management, was teaching at the University of California at San Diego, did private counseling and yoga classes, had directed and taught the Ananda Yoga Teacher Training Course, and had hosted a six-month television show on stress management.

These accomplishments sound great on paper, but I deeply felt the cost of a nonstop, hectic pace. I had gradually let go of quiet time, meditation, stretching, breathing exercises, yoga, and a healthy diet. The results were objectively graphic in terms of my health. My blood pressure had skyrocketed 25 points systolic and diastolic; headaches flared on a regular basis; almost daily my lower back throbbed in pain. I was irritable, often depressed, and exhibited all the signs of an anxious, stressed personality. For example, I would interrupt people in mid-sentence, and almost always do several things at once. To top it off, I had lost my youthful looks and natural enthusiasm.

I decided to put my research, teaching, and past experience to the test. I created and practiced *The Fitness Option Program* based on stretching exercises, breathing techniques, and quiet time practices. By following the five-week program, while continuing a highly productive lifestyle, I observed the disappearance of all psychological and physical symptoms. Within five weeks my blood pressure plummeted to normal, my youthful energy reappeared, headaches and backaches vanished, and most enjoyable to Bryan, I became a calmer, happier, and warmer spouse.

*The Fitness Option Program* worked wonders for me, and has helped thousands of others. I encourage you to follow this five-week program, which will teach you how to relax at will, erase negative habits and mental anxieties, and reduce physical knots of tension. *The Fitness Option* is a concise, step-by-step, five-week course utilizing physical exercise, breathing techniques, deep relaxation skills, and what I call instant stress releasers to regain inner strength and calm and a vital perspective on life.

## What is Stress?

Our Western industrialized way of life is contributing to tension in people from all strata of society. It has become a truism that modern lives are full of stress. Fifty to one hundred years ago the major causes of death were infectious diseases. Chicken pox, small pox, polio, typhoid, measles, and diphtheria each took its toll. Improved sanitation, antibiotics, immunization, and refrigeration have brought these diseases under control. Today most major diseases are not infection- but lifestyle-related. *As much as eighty percent of all disease can be traced directly or indirectly to stress,* including such ailments as tension and migraine headaches, muscle cramps, arthritis, digestive disorders, arteriosclerosis, cardiovascular illnesses, fatigue, depression, and anxiety. Certain disorders such as ulcers, allergies, asthma, high blood pressure, colitis, and insomnia are directly related to stress. [1,2]

**THE RESULTS IN MY OWN LIFE**
Within five weeks my blood pressure plummeted to normal, my youthful energy reappeared, headaches and backaches vanished, and most enjoyable to Bryan, I became a calmer, happier, and warmer spouse.

Stress—what is it? How does it affect us? According to Hans Seyle, renowned authority in stress research, "Stress is the response of the body to any demand made upon it. The amount of stress depends on the intensity of the demand, and the ability to cope with the demand will determine its good or bad outcome....Stress is the spice of life when it motivates us to achieve more...stress can also defeat us and cause 'distress' when we are overcome by it."[3] Stress as distress is a "subtle, constant, and unrelenting experience of anxiety due to an almost unconscious perception of threat or danger."[4]

## Physiology of Stress

How are environmental factors, thoughts, and emotions translated into physiological responses? It is helpful to have an overview of the role of the nervous system in the body/mind interface. The function of the nervous system is communication, sending and receiving messages between the peripheral nerves and the brain. The autonomic nervous system is the silent partner that is constantly working behind the scenes, adjusting and regulating such internal functions of the body as temperature, blood pressure, pulse, and digestion. At any given moment, the autonomic nervous system will be either gearing us up for action, or gearing us down for rest and repair. Both sides of the autonomic nervous system are necessary and useful as long as they function appropriately.

Due to repeated and unrelenting stress most of us cannot down shift. Research has shown that prolonged emotional stress and anxiety produce actual tissue changes and organ dysfunction. Ongoing stress keeps us speeded up and damages our internal organs.[2] There are relaxation techniques that can correct such imbalances in the autonomic nervous system. These techniques are based on knowledge of how the hypothalamus functions. It is the connecting link between our perceptions and emotions and the autonomic nervous system.

**PROLONGED STRESS**
Research has shown that prolonged emotional stress and anxiety produce actual tissue changes and organ dysfunction.

## The Body/Mind Connection

The hypothalamus is a small cluster of cells in the brain that regulates the autonomic nervous system and the endocrine (glandular) system. The hypothalamus takes mental/emotional input and translates it into physiological responses through these systems. The hypothalamus responds to perceived stress by activating the endocrine system and stimulating the sympathetic nervous system. For example, picture a shadowy figure rapidly approaching you in a dark alley. Your body prepares for "flight or fight"—to run or to battle. In response to the perceived threat, the physiological changes activated will include increased muscle tension, increased perspiration of the palms, increased heart rate, blood pressure and breath rate, increased adrenalin secretion and brain wave activity, dilation of the arteries to large muscle groups, and decreased digestive activity. By activating the endocrine system and the autonomic nervous system, the hypothalamus appears to be a "crucial" link in the chain of events through which psychological stress produces physical reaction.[2] The fascinating aspect of this connection between the mind and the body is that the body reacts similarly whether the stressor is real or imagined. For example, when you are watching a televised chase scene heightened by threatening music, your identification with the one being chased causes your body to react as though you are the one being pursued. Your body prepares to fight or escape, even though in reality you are relaxing on the couch after a hard day's work. Alternatively, a deep relaxation technique, coupled with visualizing yourself relaxing in the sun, activates a relaxation response that reduces blood pressure, lowers heartbeat and respiration rates, and relaxes muscles.

The challenge of stress management is the constant barrage of stressful events such as traffic jams, job pressures, financial strains, relationship tensions, unemployment, unpaid bills, the rising crime rate, even the threat of nuclear destruction. We give ourselves little opportunity to release the built-up tension.

In addition, the sympathetic nervous system is not activated by worry, anxiety, or strain alone. People are under pressure every time they are required to adapt or adjust to personal or environmental influences, positive or negative. Such negative stressors as in-law troubles, sexual difficulties, high mortgage payments, death of a relative, or a divorce obviously entail a gearing up to meet the demand of the situation. A birthday celebration, a vacation, a job promotion, or a marital reconciliation also require coping skills to changing environment. Extensive studies have repeatedly shown that any life change, positive or negative, produces stress.

## Stress, Illness, and the Immune System

Modern day diseases brought on by chronic tension result from an imbalance of the autonomic nervous system and endocrine system caused by our inability to manage the unrelenting onslaught of change inherent in modern living.[2] Researchers have found there is a close relationship between the amount of life changes and likelihood of future illness due to a stressful environment. Studies continue to corroborate the high correlation between number of life changes and probability of developing a major health problem. According to Doctors Holmes and Masuda, pioneer researchers in stress management, "If it takes too much effort to cope with the environment, we have less to spare for preventing disease."[5] For example, chronic stress leads to such organ malfunctions as over-secretion of gastric acid (leading to ulcers), sustained vasoconstriction (leading to hypertension), and colon hyperactivity (leading to spastic colon or colitis).

The immune system, our "first line of defense" against infection, germs, bacteria, and toxins in our bodies, is weakened by

**STRESS AND ILLNESS**
"If it takes too much effort to cope with the environment, we have less to spare for preventing disease."[5]

stress. The immune system's neurotransmitters, lymphokines, and endorphins, which are stimulated to help promote healing when the body is injured, are inhibited by stress. Fear, depression, anger, and other negative emotions depress the immune system, and long- and short-term stress can affect its vitality. Bereavement, depression, loneliness, and chronic stress reduce the natural killer cells within the immune system. According to Norman Cousins, panic burdens the heart by constricting blood vessels, and depression can open the doors to illness or intensify existing illnesses. In a study involving 75 malignant-melanoma patients, researchers at the U.C.L.A. medical center discovered that a direct link exists between the mental state of a patient and the functioning of the immune system. Severe emotions impair the immune system, while release from panic and despair frequently increase interleukins, vital substances in the immune system that help activate cancer-killing immune cells. [6]

Due to constant stress, our autonomic nervous system and endocrine system have gotten stuck in overdrive, thus inhibiting our immune system. We have overtaxed and misused our other systems by lack of exercise, improper diet, and insufficient sleep. Should we be surprised by the resulting illnesses and pain? Let's not stop on this negative note! We can make non-time-consuming changes in our lives and learn coping skills to ameliorate the pressures of stress and reduce the probability of illness.

## Psychology of Stress

The answer to managing stress lies largely in changing our perception: of ourselves and life around us. The way we perceive a situation is more important than the situation itself. Today constant change is a given in our lives, but our thoughts and feelings play a significant role in mediating the degree of distress this change causes. Plainly stated, our thoughts and attitudes affect our health. The correlation between a very stress-filled life and probability of illness is influenced by how we respond, or perceive life's changes.

Diet and exercise alone are not enough for fitness and well-being. *Stress is not just a result; it is a cause. It is not just a product; it produces.* When you connect with people and situations from the periphery of yourself, from your anger, frustration, or depression, it causes a chain reaction very different from one where you respond from an inner strength, confidence, or sense of calm. Dig beneath the layers of your outer circumstances to observe how your thought patterns and attitudes frame your life in stress. If you can see beneath the crippling personal attitudes that cause stress, you will discover a core of peace and strength. You may have forgotten this inner core of yourself; possibly you have lost touch with it. The golden glow of your life may have become tarnished with repetitious, pointless thoughts, anxious emotions, tense muscles, and the stress-related illnesses which result from them. The object of this book is to help you step out of the rut of habitual responses that trap you in a life of stress. Approaching life calmly, with dynamic yet controlled energy, will enhance your potential by reducing the illnesses or tensions that result from stress-related attitudes and emotions. The following story illustrates my point that you have a CHOICE between a life of well-being and one of stress.

Some years ago, while Bryan and I were living in the Sierra Nevada foothills, a raccoon caused havoc by upturning the trash and vandalizing our root cellar. Because that region is commonly frequented by these bushy-tailed "masked bandits," we had set out a Have-a-Heart trap. This wonderful device entices an animal into a cage with a morsel of food and the triggered door shuts behind him. One evening we baited the trap with a crisp, peanut butter filled lettuce leaf. The next morning—success! This clever, and humorously dexterous, animal had been caught red-handed, outside the cage, with his arm stretched through the bars, clutching the food in his fist. His arm was raw where he had tried to extract the culinary treasure through the bars. Had it been his nature to assess the situation with more common sense, he could have simply released the food and scampered off to freedom. He was determined to hold on tightly. We then hoisted the raccoon-adorned cage into our pick-up and drove it to a location further out in the country, where we released him from his self-imposed bondage.

How very similar we are to the raccoon! Instead of lettuce leaves, we cling to our negative moods, poor habits, and mental anxieties no matter how much they hurt us. Like the raccoon, we are rubbed the wrong way by choosing to continue in negative patterns which limit the expression of our highest potential and constrict our happiness. *The Fitness Option Program* is your opportunity to remove stress producing attitudes, habits, and perceptions which prohibit excellence in productivity and health and enjoyment of life itself.

**HABITS AND STRESS**
We cling to our negative moods, poor habits, and mental anxieties no matter how much they hurt us.

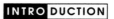

# THE SOLUTION:
# THE FITNESS OPTION PROGRAM

FORTUNATELY WE CAN DO SOMETHING about stress. We can make changes in ourselves, in our lifestyles, and in our perceptions. We can ameliorate the risks and conditions of illness. The purpose of this book is to help you bring your systems into balance. The goal is to learn to be able to relax, to regain the ability to gear up or gear down as is fitting to the situation, and to be able to control thoughts enough to lessen worries at will. The physiology of stress—the interaction of thoughts, emotions, and physical systems—indicates the need for a holistic approach to stress management. This program, *The Fitness Option,* is a holistic course that addresses the multifaceted nature of stress.

The course is a comprehensive self-help procedure for relieving tensions, incorporating up-to-date Western expertise and time-tested, research-validated Eastern techniques. Each week's instructions provide practical step-by-step guidance on incorporating the skills learned in the program into your lifestyle (which most likely has no time allowance for a separate stress management routine). *This captures the essence of the program: how to manage stress without its becoming a time-consuming endeavor.* One day at a time, you can integrate tension-relieving techniques into your life to help you live up to your fullest potential, while attaining optimal health. The course is designed to give you the opportunity to reconnect with your own inner strength and peace. It offers the means to carry your regained serenity into the seeming chaos of your life.

## The Five-Week Program

The next five chapters, *Part II*, detail the five-week course. Each week begins with a weekly lesson which presents information on one of the approaches to stress management used in the program; for example, *Week One's* lesson discusses the physiology of breathing and the effects of stress on your breath, and week two's lesson explains how to stretch correctly to reduce the physical and emotional tensions locked in your muscles. A perceptual exercise is next. These "instant stress releasers" help you understand and change your personal stress patterns. Because these are perceptual exercises, they take no time from your busy day. In fact, they help you better utilize your energy by showing you how to release unwanted tensions and mental distractions.

The weekly stress-reducing breathing technique, physical exercises, and deep relaxation are next. From personal experience and observation of countless students, I discovered the powerful effect of starting an exercise routine with breathing exercises. Each week's routine begins with a different breathing exercise, each one designed to bring your attention into the present. You will learn how to relieve such constricting emotions as fear and anxiety by application of specific breathing exercises. If you experience stress as anxiety or fatigue, there are breathing techniques to calm or revitalize you.

After the breathing exercises, each weekly routine features physical exercises to release muscular tensions. I have combined static stretching and contraction/relaxation techniques to maximize reduction of tension. These physical exercises are then followed by deep relaxation procedures, including Jacobson's Progressive Muscle Relaxation technique. Modified versions of this approach are among the most widely taught relaxation techniques in the country today. The sequence of breathing, exercise, and then conscious relaxation is important. In my research I found that my clients and students could attain deeper levels of reduced physical and emotional tension by practicing in this order.

The fourth aspect of the program is "quiet time," a term which encompasses techniques to specifically quiet restless, unproductive thought patterns. One form of quiet time, meditation, is widely appreciated for its psychological, emotional, and mental benefits. Health professionals throughout the United States teach meditation for stress reduction. Meditation significantly reduces high blood pressure and eases migraine headaches, backaches, and other symptoms of stress, if practiced a minimum of ten minutes daily.[7,8] I have included creative adaptations of meditation to give you the benefits of meditation in a personalized form.

Each chapter concludes with a Weekly Review which includes a summary of the weekly lesson, an "At-A-Glance" illustrated review of the exercises, a chart to mark your daily practice, and a space to record your comments and weekly reward for your progress.

## Personalized Stress Management

The four chapters of *Part III* are designed to meet your special needs. The first, *Stress and Your Lower Back*, discusses how to keep your back healthy and has specific exercises for those who suffer from lower back problems. The second, *Advanced Stretching and Strengthening Exercises*, is for you if you are already flexible or would like to progress to a more advanced physical routine for releasing stress and increasing flexibility. The third chapter in *Part III, Stretching 9 to 5*, has exercises to practice at the office. The fourth, *Exercises By Muscle Group*, has a chart and list of all the exercises organized by muscle group.

# HOW TO USE THIS BOOK

## Maximize Benefits of the Fitness Option Program

The routines are twenty minutes long, encompassing ten minutes of breathing and exercise, and ten minutes of deep relaxation or meditation. Exercises for the shoulders, neck, and lower back are emphasized because these are areas where many people experience tension. Because diaphragmatic breathing and the other breathing techniques are so beneficial, they are incorporated into the exercises.

A. *Practice* each of the five routines for a week. If possible, practice daily. If not, go through the twenty-minute routine at the beginning of the week and then *integrate* as much of the routine as you can into your regular day. One approach is to do the exercises and breathing in the morning and then use the relaxation or meditation in the evening. Guidelines are given on how to stretch, breathe, and consciously relax throughout the day.

B. *Start each practice* by sitting in a chair and closing your eyes. Observe how your body feels and the state of your mind. End your practice by closing your eyes and observing the results. If you find an exercise too difficult, stay with a similar one from an earlier routine. *Part III, Chapter One has an alternate routine for anyone with a weak lower back.* If your physical situation warrants it, or you are at the office, use a chair for the exercises. Consult with your physician if you have any questions, have a current illness, or have had recent surgery.

C. *While exercising,* come to the comfortable edge of the muscle's capability by moving slowly, keeping your attention on the area being stretched or strengthened. Stretching and strengthening are like shaving: Push too hard and you cut yourself, don't push hard enough and nothing happens.

D. *As you practice,* keep your focus on the exercises at hand. Make a point of bringing the mind into the activity. Use the breathing to aid your concentration.

E. *Correct alignment* of the spine and attention on protecting the joints while stretching are essential. All the exercises incorporate these concepts. For example, in a forward stretch, bending with a curled spine strains the back, and locking the knees weakens the knee joints. To flatten the back for correct alignment, bend forward from the hips, not the waist. To clarify this point, the first week's routine will emphasize correct posture. The concepts of this position are to be maintained throughout the exercises.

F. *Good posture,* deep, relaxed breathing, and keeping your attention on the present activity are fundamental behavioral tools for reducing stress.

G. *ENJOY* the routines. They are a recess from life's pressures and an intermission for you to do something nice for yourself. Make it a pleasurable break. You will feel like a new person for having taken the time.

H. *Chart* your daily progress in stress management on the chart provided at the end of each chapter.

**INCORRECT POSTURE IN THE STRETCH**
1) Hunched shoulders
2) Curled lower back
3) Locked knees

## Safety Features

As a safety feature, the routines consist of both strengthening and stretching exercises. A strong but inflexible muscle limits the range of motion of a joint and can lead to misalignment. The psoas muscles are a case in point. These muscles, attached to the front of each vertebra of the lumbar spine, extend across the hip joint and attach to the thigh. Each time you bend the knee toward the chest, as in walking or jogging, you use these muscles to raise the thigh. Repeated contraction of the muscles increases their strength but also shortens them. The shortening of these muscles, if they are not stretched out regularly, pulls the lumbar spine down and forward and possibly out of alignment.

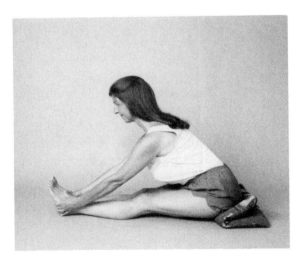

**CORRECT POSTURE IN THE STRETCH**
1) Neck, shoulders, and spine in correct alignment
2) Knees straight, not locked
3) Forward stretch from hips, not waist

**YOU ARE IN CONTROL**
Stress management is in your hands. You can change your life from one of continuing anxiety and tension to one of challenge and well-being.

The other side of the coin is to have flexibility but insufficient strength. In this case, you may have the full range of motion of the joint, but lack the muscular strength to keep the vertebrae of the spine or a joint in alignment. For example, forward bending stretches out the extensors at the back of the spine, but the forward bending needs to be balanced with back arching exercises that strengthen the muscles and ligaments which hold the spine upright. Keep this in mind as you exercise: the balance between flexibility and strength. You need both. Each week's routine establishes this crucial balance.

The exercise routines also maintain a balance between energizing and calming you. Upon completion you will feel peaceful yet vitalized. You will feel less stressed because of reduced muscular and mental tension. You will be more alert and energetic because of released emotional strain, improved circulation, increased oxygen supply, and efficient carbon dioxide removal. The result will be a healthier, more relaxed you.

Stress management is in your hands. You can change your life from one of continuing anxiety and tension to one of challenge and well-being. This five-week stress management course will enable you to make changes in your life and to live with a greater sense of peace.

## Results of Practicing The Fitness Option Program

What are the results of practicing the techniques taught in the program? I have taught this course in shortened and extended versions for over twenty years with overwhelming affirmative feedback from students. (See front page of this book.) Testimonials of reduced tensions and increased vitality are supported by independent research. For example, in a study I conducted using a matched control group, subjects followed this course for three weeks and experienced significant reduction in stress symptomology as measured by pulse, blood pressure, respiration, and a stress symptoms checklist. A follow-up study one month later revealed continued reduction of stress symptomology for those who continued to put into practice the ideas and exercises of this program. [9]

# MEASURING YOUR LEVEL OF STRESS

THE FOLLOWING STRESS TESTS are included to help you become aware of your level of stress and how you express your tensions. Take the tests now and save your scores. At the end of the five-week course, retake the tests to see your improvement. Duplicates of these tests are at the end of *Week Five*.

## How to Evaluate the Results of the Stress Tests

The stress symptoms checklists are to help you to be aware of how you experience stress and to evaluate the relative intensity of your stress. Everyone needs coping skills to handle life's pressures and this program gives you a holistic approach to stress management. If your stress symptoms continue, consider seeing a professional trained in psychological counseling or a physician who can give you personal guidance.

Because tests need to be standardized to meet the criteria of large numbers of people, these tests may not totally apply to you. Within this context, look at the results as guidelines for your stress management. For example, do you experience stress more physically or emotionally?

Are your psychological responses to stress more the high-energy emotions such as anger, hostility, or restlessness, or the low-energy emotions such as depression, boredom, or a sense of hopelessness? You will want to match your results with the appropriate tools for managing stress. Low-energy emotional responses to stress imply the need to practice the breathing exercises given in *Week Four* and *Week Five* and a few of the gentle physical exercises, and to look at re-evaluating your perceptions of yourself and life's challenges. See *Week Four* for more information on changing your perceptions. When you're under stress, if you can, get outside, especially into nature, and take a walk in the park or along the beach. Call or visit a friend. These activities get you outside your downward cycle and expand your view. When we stay inside and alone, our problems seem bigger than ourselves. When you are feeling low-energy emotions it is best not to do deep relaxation or to meditate. You will not want to do high-energy activities either, so begin to get your energy going in small, incremental steps.

If you are experiencing the high-energy emotions, you have too much energy to focus on the more subtle tools of stress management. If you can, go for a brisk walk or jog, or let off steam by engaging in a sport you enjoy. Practice several rounds of *The Sun Salutation* given in *Part III, Chapter Two*. If you are short on time, take six *Three-Part Rhythmic Breaths* as taught in *Week Three*. Later in the day try reevaluating the situation from a calmer perspective.

Review the checklist on your physical responses to stress to see if you can see any patterns. For example, do you experience stress as cardiovascular symptoms? Do you have a family history of weakness in a given area? Choose stress management tools appropriate to your situation.

Do you experience stress manifesting in stomach and digestive disorders? Perhaps you need to look at your eating patterns. *Week Five* gives nutritional tools for stress management.

Do you hold tension in your shoulders and neck? Focus on the exercises given each week for the neck and shoulders. Do not wait until the end of eight hours of desk work to do the exercises. Every thirty minutes, or at your breaks, do two or three of the exercises to avoid a build-up of tension. Take a look at *Part III, Chapter Three* on exercises for the office.

Use the tests to pinpoint how you experience stress and then use *The Fitness Option Program* as a guide for helping you manage your stress.

# O'HARA STRESS INDICATOR CHECKLIST
## PSYCHOLOGICAL RESPONSES TO STRESS

CIRCLE THE NUMBER WHICH BEST DESCRIBES the frequency of the occurrence of the following indicators of stress, and total your score.

|  | Seldom | Infrequent (not more than once a month) | Occasional (more than once per month) | Very Often (more than once per week) | Constant |
|---|---|---|---|---|---|
| Depression | 1 | 2 | 3 | 4 | 5 |
| Sense of hopelessness | 1 | 2 | 3 | 4 | 5 |
| Feeling of powerlessness | 1 | 2 | 3 | 4 | 5 |
| Low self-esteem | 1 | 2 | 3 | 4 | 5 |
| Frustration | 1 | 2 | 3 | 4 | 5 |
| Anger | 1 | 2 | 3 | 4 | 5 |
| Irritability | 1 | 2 | 3 | 4 | 5 |
| Resentment | 1 | 2 | 3 | 4 | 5 |
| Hostility | 1 | 2 | 3 | 4 | 5 |
| Anxiety in relationships | 1 | 2 | 3 | 4 | 5 |
| Anxiety over deadlines | 1 | 2 | 3 | 4 | 5 |
| Fearfulness | 1 | 2 | 3 | 4 | 5 |
| Boredom | 1 | 2 | 3 | 4 | 5 |
| Restlessness | 1 | 2 | 3 | 4 | 5 |

**TOTAL SCORE:**

**SCORE INTERPRETATION:**
**14-25** Comfortable handling stress ◆ **26-35** Could sharpen coping skills
**36-60** Time for changes ◆ **Over 60** Uncomfortable handling stress

# O'HARA STRESS SYMPTOMS CHECKLIST
## PHYSICAL RESPONSES TO STRESS

CIRCLE THE NUMBER WHICH BEST DESCRIBES the frequency of occurrence of the following symptoms, and then total your score.

| | Seldom | Infrequent (not more than once a month) | Occasional (more than once per month) | Very Often (more than once per week) | Constant |
|---|---|---|---|---|---|
| Migraine headache | 1 | 2 | 3 | 4 | 5 |
| Tension headache | 1 | 2 | 3 | 4 | 5 |
| Clammy hands/feet | 1 | 2 | 3 | 4 | 5 |
| Rapid shallow breath | 1 | 2 | 3 | 4 | 5 |
| Tightness in chest | 1 | 2 | 3 | 4 | 5 |
| Heart pounding | 1 | 2 | 3 | 4 | 5 |
| High blood pressure | 1 | 2 | 3 | 4 | 5 |
| Diarrhea | 1 | 2 | 3 | 4 | 5 |
| Constipation | 1 | 2 | 3 | 4 | 5 |
| Burping | 1 | 2 | 3 | 4 | 5 |
| Gassiness | 1 | 2 | 3 | 4 | 5 |
| Colitis | 1 | 2 | 3 | 4 | 5 |
| Increased urge to urinate | 1 | 2 | 3 | 4 | 5 |
| Indigestion | 1 | 2 | 3 | 4 | 5 |
| Backache | 1 | 2 | 3 | 4 | 5 |
| Neck pain | 1 | 2 | 3 | 4 | 5 |
| Dry mouth | 1 | 2 | 3 | 4 | 5 |
| Muscular tension | 1 | 2 | 3 | 4 | 5 |
| Sleeping difficulties | 1 | 2 | 3 | 4 | 5 |
| Fatigue | 1 | 2 | 3 | 4 | 5 |
| Dizziness | 1 | 2 | 3 | 4 | 5 |
| Menstrual distress | 1 | 2 | 3 | 4 | 5 |
| Ulcers | 1 | 2 | 3 | 4 | 5 |
| Tics/tremors | 1 | 2 | 3 | 4 | 5 |
| Jaw pain/tension | 1 | 2 | 3 | 4 | 5 |
| Skin rash | 1 | 2 | 3 | 4 | 5 |
| Asthma | 1 | 2 | 3 | 4 | 5 |
| Allergy | 1 | 2 | 3 | 4 | 5 |
| Gum chewing | 1 | 2 | 3 | 4 | 5 |
| Teeth grinding | 1 | 2 | 3 | 4 | 5 |
| Procrastinating | 1 | 2 | 3 | 4 | 5 |
| Irregular eating habits | 1 | 2 | 3 | 4 | 5 |
| Clenching fists | 1 | 2 | 3 | 4 | 5 |
| Nail biting | 1 | 2 | 3 | 4 | 5 |
| Rapid/loud talking | 1 | 2 | 3 | 4 | 5 |
| Emotional overreaction | 1 | 2 | 3 | 4 | 5 |
| Failure to complete projects | 1 | 2 | 3 | 4 | 5 |
| Doing several things simultaneously | 1 | 2 | 3 | 4 | 5 |

**TOTAL SCORE:**

**SCORE INTERPRETATION:**
**38-60** Comfortable handling stress ◆ **61-80** Could sharpen coping skills
**81-125** Time for changes ◆ **Over 125** Uncomfortable handling stress

# PART II

# THE FIVE-WEEK
# FITNESS OPTION PROGRAM

*Rooted in peace, the flower of our potential blooms in the light of life's challenges.*

WEEK ONE

## LESSON ONE: BREATHING TECHNIQUES FOR STRESS MANAGEMENT

BREATHE FULLY AND DEEPLY. Draw in the life-giving oxygen about you. Life begins and ends with breath. This overlooked part of ourselves is basic to our survival, fundamental to our well-being. The foundation of stress management is proper breathing habits. By breathing correctly you can alter your response to life. You will learn how to convert fatigue into vitality and restlessness into calmness. To increase your level of energy, the program teaches you to breathe more efficiently and to expand your lung capacity. To decrease your level of tension it gives breathing exercises to calm the nervous system and quiet the mind.

Oxygen is vital to our survival. Rather than enhancing the input of this live-giving energy, we sit and stand in cramped postures, reducing the quantity of oxygen in our lungs. We further inhibit our oxygen intake with shallow breathing, filling only the top portion of our lungs. We are cutting off our very life supply.

Yawning can indicate that you are not breathing correctly. It is not only a function of boredom or fatigue, but is also the body's means of drawing in needed oxygen. Often, we forget to contract our abdominal muscles and completely exhale, thereby leaving stale air in our lower lungs. We need to learn how to correctly inhale and exhale to maximize use of oxygen and removal of carbon dioxide.

Take a moment to observe your breath. How are you breathing? What is the rhythm and depth of your breath? With thought and training you can enhance your life by altering your breathing patterns.

### Physiology of Breathing

The amount of carbon dioxide versus the amount of oxygen in the blood is monitored by the reticular activating system in the medulla

**BREATHING HABITS**
The foundation of stress management is proper breathing habits. By breathing correctly you can alter your response to life.

at the base of the brain. Upon registering a deficiency in oxygen, this system sends nerve impulses to the intercostal muscles between the ribs to expand, and to the diaphragm, a powerful dome-shaped muscle which divides the thorasic cavity above from the abdominal cavity below, to contract downward. The resulting expansion in the chest causes a partial vacuum and an imbalance in pressure between the air sacs within the lungs and the air around us. As a result air is drawn into the lungs (inhalation). Oxygen transverses the lungs via "leaky" capillaries to the arteries, blood vessels which carry the oxygen to the body's cells. Oxygen is then used as fuel for each cell to carry out its designated function. The by-product or waste, carbon dioxide, is carried away by the veins to the heart and then the lungs, and out of the body through exhalation.

The descending movement of the diaphragm provides an internal massage and stimulation to the liver, stomach, spleen, kidneys, adrenals, pancreas, colon, and other viscera, which is crucial to their normal functioning. When we inhibit movement of the diaphragm by poor posture, tense abdominal muscles or poor breathing habits, we interfere with the normal functioning of the digestive, eliminative, and assimilating systems. [10]

The unique aspect of the breathing system is that it can be either automatic or controlled because it is connected to both the involuntary (unconscious) and the voluntary (conscious) nervous systems. The breath is self-regulating, yet at the same time we can choose to become aware of the breath and consciously control or alter the rhythm of our breath. By consciously changing the rhythm of the breath, we can affect our mood and level of vitality. We can choose to slow down and deepen the breath, or practice one of the energizing breaths.

One of the benefits of conscious breathing is to learn how to increase lung capacity so that we can draw in a larger supply of oxygen. This not only gives us more energy in our daily lives, but is excellent for more strenuous activities or sports. A major portion of the lungs consists of minute balloons, one-membrane-thick air sacs called alveolii. If you spread the alveolii out on the floor one membrane high, they would cover the area of a football field! To increase lung capacity means learning how to consciously stretch the respiratory muscles encasing the lungs. This entails learning how to stretch or relax such respiratory muscles as the diaphragm, the intercostal muscles between the ribs, the muscles connecting the twelfth rib to the pelvis, the relevant muscles of the neck, and the muscles in the upper, middle, and lower back. All these muscles can be stretched during a complete inhalation to maximize the space available to the alveolii during inhalation.

We can also control what portion of the lungs we fill. There are more blood vessels in the lower portion of the lungs than in the upper portion; therefore, to maximize the oxygen/carbon dioxide exchange we need to fill the lower section of our lungs. Watch a sleeping baby and observe the gentle rise and fall of the abdominal area. With each inhalation the baby's abdominal muscles relax; with

**THE CONSCIOUS CONTROL OF BREATH**
We can choose to become aware of the breath and consciously control or alter the rhythm of our breath. By consciously changing the rhythm of the breath, we can affect our mood and level of vitality.

each exhalation the abdominal muscles contract. This natural process allows room for the diaphragm to move up and down during the breathing process. During inhalation, as the diaphragm contracts (pulling down), the abdominal muscles relax forward, allowing for expansion of the lower lungs. During exhalation, as the diaphragm moves upward, the abdominal muscles contract, helping to expel the stale air (carbon dioxide) from the lower lungs.

Many of us, especially women, have learned to override this natural, healthy process. In an attempt to look fashionably thin, people keep their abdominal muscles contracted, inhibiting the air flow to the lower portion of the lungs.

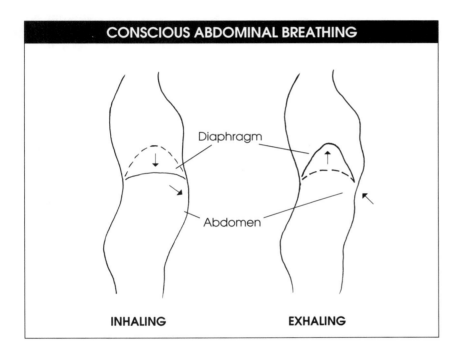

## CONSCIOUS ABDOMINAL BREATHING

Diaphragm

Abdomen

INHALING                    EXHALING

## Emotions and The Breath

How do you breathe when you are relaxed? How do you breathe when you are at peace with yourself and the world? Abdominal or diaphragmatic breathing, which you will learn this week, is the natural way of breathing when you are relaxed. Compare this slow, rhythmic breathing with the shallow, fast, erratic breathing which accompanies anger, fear, or anxiety. Some people, when nervous or tense, tighten the abdominal muscles, restricting the flow of oxygen. This exacerbates stress symptoms such as indigestion and constipation.

Experience the following visualizations. Take several minutes imagining yourself in a calm, serene place in nature and then observe your breath and any tension in your body. Next, take several minutes visualizing an aspect of your life where there is tension, perhaps inharmony in a relationship or in the work place. Experience

Anxiety inhibits the flow of oxygen to the brain by causing the blood vessels to constrict. The limited oxygen supply to the brain reduces clarity of thought.

that aspect of your life and listen to the words you or others are speaking, then observe your breath and any tension in your body. Take a deep breath and release this aspect of your life. Did you notice the difference in your breath in these two situations? Just as your emotions affect your breath, so you can use the breath to change an emotion.

Stress also affects one's ability to think clearly. How many times do we forget a friend's name or the name of a business associate when under the pressure of conducting introductions? Over 50% of our oxygen supply is utilized by the brain. Anxiety inhibits the flow of oxygen to the brain by causing the blood vessels to constrict. The limited oxygen supply to the brain reduces clarity of thought.

The stress management program tackles the challenge of incorrect breathing habits. For example, diaphragmatic breathing teaches you how to change your pattern of breathing from shallow, upper lung breathing to lower lung breathing. This is the way you should be breathing a majority of the time.

The *Complete Breath,* which is taught in the second week of the program, is useful in stressful situations. It has a calming effect and can be practiced at any time. This technique is taught by health practitioners to help control anxiety attacks and is utilized by asthmatics whose symptoms are stress related.

Recently a student came to me for help during an asthmatic attack coupled with an anxiety attack. Because of the severity of the situation, she could not use her inhaler. She was deeply frightened and could barely gasp for air because of constriction and spasming of the bronchial tubes. Rather than going to the hospital, as she had in previous situations, she practiced the *Diaphragmatic Breath* and the *Complete Breath*. Within ten minutes these breathing techniques plus consciously relaxing her muscles had restored her natural breathing rhythm and quelled her fear.

Before an interview, lecture, or performance the *Three-Part Rhythmic Breath* presented in *Week Three* helps one calm the fears and nervousness, while the energizing breathing techniques of *Weeks Four* and *Five* help you if you lack energy.

# INSTANT STRESS RELEASER

### Integrating Diaphragmatic Breathing Into Your Day

During this first week of the program, practice the following two stress releasers:

1. Start integrating diaphragmatic breathing into your day (see the following section for detailed instructions). Experience its effect on your level of tension. The slow rhythmic breathing is calming and relaxing. To make it your natural way of breathing, begin by observing your breathing at relatively stress-free times during the day. Start breathing diaphragmatically if you find you are not doing so already. For example, observe yourself while doing simple tasks at the office or at home. If you are not breathing diaphragmatically, do so. Gradually expand the times of practice until it is your natural way of breathing.

2. Periodically observe yourself for bodily tension. See if you can catch yourself clenching your jaw, tensing your shoulders, grasping your hands, or other such physical expressions of tension. Once you are aware of the tension, briefly exaggerate the tension by tensing more deeply in the designated muscles. Relax, and feel the difference between the tension and the relaxation. Repeat two more times, tensing and relaxing the area and comparing the difference. Follow this with three slow *Diaphragmatic Breaths,* and on the exhalation relax more deeply in the problem area. Feel as if you are breathing space into the area. This instant stress releaser helps you to become aware of how and where you hold tension and gives you a tool for releasing the tension.

**TO DO**
This week start practicing diaphragmatic breathing each day. Also, periodically check yourself for bodily tension.

# BREATHING EXERCISE

### Diaphragmatic Breath

This simple but powerful breathing technique consists of breathing slowly, filling only the lower portion of the lungs by relaxing the abdominal muscles while inhaling, and contracting the abdominal muscles while exhaling. Diaphragmatic breathing activates the lower portions of the lungs while the middle and upper portions of the lungs are passive. The breathing is through the nose, not the mouth.

Begin by stretching out on your back on the carpet or a mat. Take time to relax and let go of tensions. Focus on your legs and relax them. Next, concentrate on the trunk of your body and relax the buttocks, chest, and back muscles. Relax your arms from the shoulders down to the finger tips, and then bring your attention to your neck and facial muscles and feel a letting go of tensions there. Become conscious of the weight of your body against the carpet, and relax more deeply. After taking several minutes to do

These exercises can be done any time: in the morning, in your car, at work or school, or in the evening.

this, concentrate in the abdominal area and observe the movement there as you breathe. Does the abdomen rise as you inhale and contract as you exhale? This is the natural process you are seeking.

Place a book over your navel. As you inhale, push the abdominal muscles (and the book) toward the ceiling. As you exhale, contract the abdominal muscles toward the carpet and observe the book lower toward your spine. Repeat this three times. Now repeat the exercise, but relax the abdominal muscles rather than pushing them as you inhale. The pushing is just an initial practice to better understand the exercise.

Remove the book and take a long inhalation to the count of four (or a number comfortable to you) and then exhale to an equal count. Be sure to keep the rib cage and upper chest passive. Practice this slow breathing several times.

Come into a comfortable seated position and repeat the process using your hand over your navel. Take three breaths, pushing the navel and your hand out as you inhale and then consciously contracting the abdominal muscles as your exhale.

Release your hand and now relax the abdominal muscles as you inhale, still consciously contracting the abdominal muscles as you exhale. Repeat the breath in a slow, even rhythm, with the rib cage and upper lungs remaining passive. This is diaphragmatic breathing.

Begin this week's routine with six, slow *Diaphragmatic Breaths,* three lying down, and three sitting up. This form of breathing is also practiced in all the exercises. Diaphragmatically inhale and exhale slowly and deeply as you go into and out of the stretches, and while you hold a position. On each exhalation allow yourself to relax more deeply into the stretched position.

# WEEK ONE ROUTINE

Diaphragmatic Breaths

Standing Posture

Neck Rolls

Shoulder Shrugs

Palm Press

The Rag Doll

Chest Expander

The Cat

Seated Side Stretch

Spinal Twist on Back, Legs Crossed

Full Body Stretch

Active Deep Relaxation

FIRST READ THE INSTRUCTIONS and practice all of the exercises. Then use the At-A-Glance in the Weekly Review section at the end of each chapter as a reminder of all the exercises. During the week integrate the exercises into your day if the ten minutes of exercises and the ten minutes of deep relaxation are too time-consuming for you.

It is easy to fit the relaxation exercises into your day once you experiment with them. For example, the breathing exercises can be done any time. When you first get up in the morning, try *The Cat* series and a *Seated Side Stretch*. Do the chair series at the kitchen sink or in the bathroom. Some *Neck Rolls* and *Shoulder Shrugs* are easily practiced while waiting at a red light. A *Palm Press* and several *Shoulder Shrugs* are a beneficial break when your neck and shoulders are tense from long hours at a desk. After a long day, *The Rag Doll* and a *Spinal Twist on Back, Legs Crossed* feel great. Take a moment to tense and relax the body parts, as in *Active Deep Relaxation*, just before going to sleep.

The breathing, stretching, and relaxing do make a difference. The instant stress releasers are of further benefit. The key to each of these brief relaxation skills is to practice regularly, breath slowly, concentrate, and relax in the process. They can become an approach to life, an integral part of your day, not a separate time-consuming process.

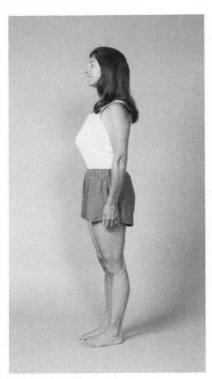

Standing Posture

## DETAILED INSTRUCTIONS ON WEEK ONE EXERCISES

BEFORE BEGINNING THE FIVE WEEKS OF EXERCISES and relaxation, consult your physician if you have an illness or injury, or have had surgery recently. If you have a weak lower back, see *Part III*, for alternate exercises. All of the routines are gentle, but do take any necessary precautions.

### Diaphragmatic Breath

Practice three *Diaphragmatic Breaths* lying down and three *Diaphragmatic Breaths* sitting on the floor or in a chair.

### Standing Posture

Assume your best posture, feet parallel, one inch apart. Distribute your weight evenly on your feet. Focus on your knees and be sure not to hyperextend the knee joints. This means not locking your knees by pushing back on them. Instead, gently unhinge them approximately ½-inch. Rather than pushing back on the knees, gently lift up at the kneecaps and thighs. This protects the knees, and also helps keep correct alignment of the lower back.

To feel the effect on your lower back, place your hands on your back at your waist with the fingers pointing towards the carpet. Lock your knees and feel what happens in your back. Then, unhinge your knees, keeping them straight but not locked, and feel the difference in your lower back. Hyperextended knees and a tense, over-arched back go together. Change your knees and help both areas.

Now place your hands on your hips, hands around your waist, with the fingers going forward and the thumbs toward your back. Holding there attempt to lengthen the torso area. Lift up out of your hips. Feel like a plant growing. Another image is of a Spanish dancer, hands on hips, torso elongated. There is a lifting up from the pelvis through the chest, and a sense of relaxing down in the back from the waist.

Feel open and expansive in the chest area. Experiment with visualizing a rose blossom opening at the heart. Part of poor posture, especially in the chest area, is an attitude of distrust and fear of life, a closing off to the harsh realities around us. If you can stand with an attitude of being open to life's challenges, it will affect your posture (and how people respond to you).

Relax your shoulders, and lengthen the neck the way you did the torso. Keep the chin parallel to the floor.

With these ideas in mind, practice standing again, but this time in front of a mirror. Make any needed adjustments. Add diaphragmatic breathing. Once you have these basics the rest falls into place. Do not be in a hurry to get to the rest of the first week's exercises. Work out the details of the *Diaphragmatic Breath* and the

### POSTURE IS THE KEY

The key to the exercises is to keep the integrity of the standing posture. To maintain the correct position of the spine when bending forward, do not bend at the waist, but from the hips.

*Standing Posture,* and then put them into practice. Observe yourself throughout the day. Correct breathing and posture are fundamental in stress management.

The concepts of the standing posture are practiced in all the exercises. Let's take a sitting forward stretch as an example. If you were to sit with your legs straight in front of you on the floor and try to touch your toes, you could strain and possibly injure your spine by forcing your head to your knees. The key to the exercises is to keep the integrity of the *Standing Posture.* To maintain the correct position of the spine when bending forward, do not bend at the waist, but from the hips. You will not go down as far, but you will stretch the back of the thighs while protecting the spine.

As in the *Standing Posture,* observe your knees to be sure they are not hyperextended during the exercises, and hold your head in correct alignment. Do not sacrifice the integrity of a correct (and safe) position for the goal of the full stretch.

The exercises can become an observing and training ground for how you approach life. As you practice notice if you are in a hurry, pushing too hard, sacrificing safety rules, or letting your mind drift to future activities.

## Neck Rolls

While standing, lift the shoulders towards your ears with your arms relaxed to your sides. Holding the shoulders up, gently drop the chin towards the chest. While inhaling, roll the head clockwise to the side and then back; while exhaling, roll the head to the other side and then forward (chin towards the chest). Repeat one more time. Relax the shoulders, and lift the head back to its normal position. Repeat the process, rolling the neck counter-clockwise.

Practicing with the shoulders lifted protects the neck, but if it feels more comfortable and you have no neck problems, practice with the shoulders relaxed in their normal position. Maintain correct posture during the neck rolls.

Neck Rolls

## Shoulder Shrugs

In the standing position, curl your shoulders forward until you feel a stretch in your upper back; your arms will relax toward the front of your body. Then lift the shoulders towards your ears. Follow this by rolling the shoulders back, feeling the shoulder blades coming together. Then pull the shoulders down until you feel a stretching across the shoulders. Think of pulling the elbows towards the floor. Repeat, this time adding diaphragmatic breathing, inhaling as you shrug your shoulders forward and then up, and exhaling as you shrug your shoulders back and then down.

Repeat the process two more times, but now reverse it by pulling the shoulders back and then up, forward and then down. Inhale as you pull back and up, exhale as you shrug forward and down.

Shoulder Shrugs

Palm Press

The Rag Doll

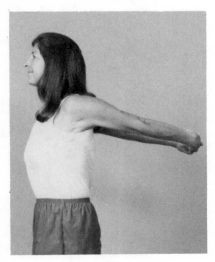

Chest Expander

## Palm Press

From the standing position, inhale, slowly raise your arms out to the side to shoulder height, your palms facing down; exhale, stretching from your chest through your fingertips. Hold, arms extended, for one breath, extending sideways as far as you can to maximize the stretch in the shoulders and chest. Do not push the shoulder blades together. Then continue raising the arms, inhaling, until the hands are touching, back to back, over your head, arms by your ears. As you exhale, relax the shoulders and move the hands past each other, crossing at the wrists so that the palms are now touching each other. Keeping this position, inhale, stretching through the arms. Then holding the breath for as long as you can without straining, press the palms together. Exhale, maintaining the position, but relaxing the pressure of the palms and the shoulders. Repeat the inhaling, holding the breath and palm pressing, and then exhaling and relaxing two more times. Separate the arms so that they are parallel over your head. Inhale and stretch the arms up towards the ceiling and back; exhale and slowly lower the arms. Gently shake your shoulders.

## The Rag Doll

Standing with correct posture, inhale. As you exhale, tuck your chin and slowly bend forward. Be loose and relaxed: the chest curled, the knees bent 3-4 inches, the arms loose. Once you are as far over as you can go, take three *Diaphragmatic Breaths* while relaxing the neck, shoulders, lower back, and backs of the thighs. Think of being loose and relaxed like a rag doll. As you stay in the position you will feel a relaxing of the muscles. Take hold of your elbows with your opposite hands to further relax the neck and shoulders. Take three more *Diaphragmatic Breaths,* relaxing more deeply with each exhalation. With a curled spine, bent knees, and tucked chin, slowly come back into the standing position; keep the chin tucked for one breath to prevent dizziness.

## Chest Expander

While standing, interlock your fingers behind you, resting them on your buttocks. As you inhale, pull down on the shoulders and arms. As you exhale, gently tuck and tighten the buttocks muscles (to protect the lower back) and raise your arms as high as they will go without straining. Hold the position at the edge of the stretch for three breaths. Lower your arms back down into the standing position.

## The Cat

**First Position:** Come down onto your hands and knees. Have your hands directly under your shoulders, with your fingers pointing forward. Have your knees directly under your hips. As you curl the

The Cat (First Position)

The Cat (Second Position)

The Cat (Third Position)

The Cat (Fourth Position)

back towards the ceiling, exhale and feel the stretch: Tighten the buttocks slightly, press on the palms with elbows straight, and tuck the chin towards the chest.

**Second Position:** As you arch the spine, inhale, relax in the lower back, and pull down and back on the shoulders (lengthening the space between the head and shoulders). Keep the elbows straight. Curl and arch the spine slowly three times.

**Third Position:** Turn the fingers toward each other and lower the chest and chin toward the floor, keeping the buttocks and elbows high. Take three *Diaphragmatic Breaths* in this position and then come back up.

**Fourth Position:** Curl the back towards the ceiling again and slowly lower the buttocks to the heels. Take three breaths in this position, stretching the lower back and spine by reaching out ahead of you with your hands on the floor. To come out of the position, bring your hands by your feet without changing your position, and tighten your abdominal muscles. With your back straight, raise your trunk into a position where you're sitting on your legs, spine erect.

Seated Side Stretch

## Seated Side Stretch

Sit in a comfortable cross-legged position. As in the *Standing Posture,* lift up out of the hips, open through the chest, and keep the chin parallel to the floor. To help keep the natural arch of the lower back, sit on the edge of a pillow. Place your right hand on the floor beside you. While inhaling, stretch your left arm, with your palm facing upward, out to the side and then all the way up towards the ceiling. Slowly exhale, bending to the right side. Hold the stretched position for three *Diaphragmatic Breaths.* As you hold the position, you will feel the muscles relax and you will be able to rest the right forearm on the carpet. Take three more slow breaths, extending deeper into the stretch with each breath. To come out of the position tighten your abdominal muscles, and lift the trunk upright with the left arm over your head. Slowly lower your arm. Repeat the stretch to the left side.

## Spinal Twist on Back, Legs Crossed

**First Position:** Stretch out on your back and bend your knees to your chest. Clasp your hands around your legs and gently stretch your lower back. Cross the left leg over the right leg at the thighs and stretch your arms out on the carpet at shoulder height with the palms against the carpet. Inhale, keeping the legs close to your chest.

**Second Position:** As you exhale, lower your legs to the right side of your body and turn your head in the opposite direction. Take six, slow *Diaphragmatic Breaths* in this position, relaxing your lower back, legs, and feet with each exhalation. Keep your knees as close to your chest as you can. On the next inhalation, bring the legs and head back to the original position. Repeat to the other side with the right leg crossed over the left leg.

Spinal Twist on Back, Legs Crossed (First Position)

Spinal Twist on Back, Legs Crossed (Second Position)

## Full Body Stretch

You will need to use props for this stretch, but it is well worth it. I enjoy this stretch at the kitchen sink every morning. Use a wall, sturdy table, or chair.

**First Position:** Place your hands on the wall (or a chair) at hip height and then walk away from the wall until your back is parallel to the floor, feet hip distance apart. Focus on stretching your spine by pressing against the wall with your hands and pushing your buttocks in the opposite direction. Extend the hands and hips in opposite directions, elongating the spine.

If your hamstrings (backs of the thighs) feel too stretched, bend the knees enough to allow the spine to stretch out from the hips, not the waist. Take three, slow *Diaphragmatic Breaths*

**Second Position:** The second phase of the exercise focuses on stretching the hamstrings and releasing tension along the spine by arching and curling. Begin by pressing down into the heels while pushing the buttocks up toward the ceiling and arching your back. Move slowly, focusing first on arching the lower back, then middle back, and finally upper back. Lift your head so that you are looking at the wall. Take three *Diaphragmatic Breaths.*

**Third Position:** Bring the spine back to the first position (a flat back) and then slowly curl your back towards the ceiling. Move slowly feeling the curl first in the lower, then middle, and then upper spine, tucking your chin to the chest. Take three *Diaphragmatic Breaths.* Repeat each position two more times.

Remember to keep the legs three feet apart and knees partially bent if it is too much of a stretch behind your thighs. Relax the legs and come out of the position.

Full Body Stretch (First Position)

Full Body Stretch (Second Position)

Full Body Stretch (Third Position)

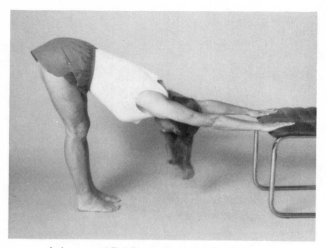

Advanced Full Body Stretch (First Position)

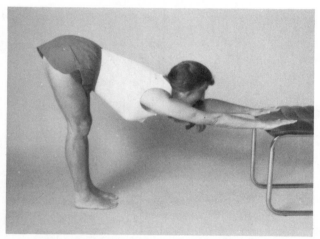

Advanced Full Body Stretch (Second Position)

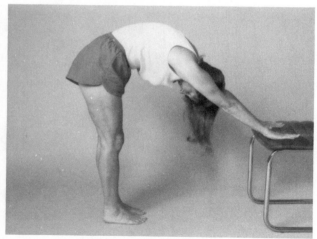

Advanced Full Body Stretch (Third Position)

## Advanced Full Body Stretch

Once you are comfortable with the first and second positions, and feel flexible enough, increase the stretch in the chest, lower back, and hamstrings by repeating the stretch with your hands lower down the wall or on the seat of a chair. First feel the spine straight and take three breaths, then begin arching the spine and holding for three breaths. Flatten the spine and then curl and hold for three breaths. Repeat the curling and arching two more times.

## How are you feeling now?

*These exercises are more than physical stretches: They release blocked emotional tension in the shoulders, spine, and legs. Students often mention feeling taller from these stretches.*

## Deep Relaxation

Deep relaxation is one of the most beneficial techniques used in stress management. It is also everyone's favorite "exercise." One student aptly called it the "dessert." One of the most well-known forms of deep relaxation is Edmond Jacobson's Progressive Muscle Relaxation (PMR). Jacobson, a pioneer in relaxation research, developed PMR to treat patients with anxiety. His purpose was to replace the use of tranquilizing agents. PMR consists of contracting and relaxing major muscle groups. This procedure, in its initial version, consists of approximately fifty one-hour sessions of relaxation training. In each session the patient lies on his back, eyes closed. After three minutes of relaxing muscles, he tenses and relaxes a specific muscle group three times. The rest of the hour he goes limp, letting the whole body relax. There is no suggestive or autosuggestive activity included. Over time the entire procedure is shortened. The purpose is to avoid inappropriate muscular tension under all conditions. [11]

Variations and shortened versions making PMR more practical have been developed, and therapists have refined the technique to meet specific therapeutic demands. It is now widely used throughout the country by therapists, counselors, and exercise physiologists to relax muscular tension and reduce anxiety and stress. The following *Active Deep Relaxation* is my ten-minute version of PMR, specifically structured to reduce muscular tensions resulting from stress.

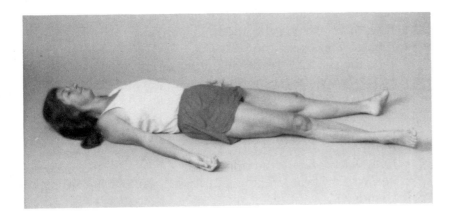

# DEEP RELAXATION

## Active Deep Relaxation

Lie on your back on a carpet or mat with your feet approximately one and one-half feet apart. Have your arms about a foot away from your body with your palms facing toward the ceiling. Close your eyes. A quiet setting with the lights off aids the process. Just as in the standing position, be sure you are in a straight line. Look towards your toes to verify your position. To release the lower back, briefly tighten your abdominal muscles and buttocks and push the small of your back towards the carpet, then relax. To adjust the neck and shoulders, briefly push the back of your neck towards the carpet by tucking your chin towards your chest and curling your shoulders towards the ceiling, and then relax. Make any adjustments you need to be comfortable.

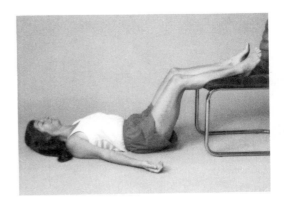

**ACTIVE DEEP RELAXATION: ALTERNATE POSTION**

If you have a weak, tense or painful lower back, it feels good to place a pillow under the thighs or rest your calves on the seat of a chair.

   **Alternate Position:** If you have a weak, tense, or painful lower back, it feels good to place a pillow under the thighs or rest your calves on the seat of a chair.

   You are now ready to begin. Starting with the feet, body parts are tensed for approximately three seconds and then relaxed. After each relaxation of a muscle group, observe the difference in sensation between the tension and the relaxation phase. To approximate three seconds, think of increasing the tension from low, to medium, to high; then release the tension. Take ten minutes to complete the whole relaxation process. Record the instructions on the next page on an audio cassette for a deeper relaxation.

## Active Deep Relaxation

**TENSE/RELAX/OBSERVE**
After tensing and then relaxing a muscle, observe the difference in sensation between the tension and relaxation phase.

◇ Point the toes and *tense/relax/observe* the feet.
◇ Flex the heels (push the heels away from you) and *tense/relax/observe* the calves and knees.
◇ *Tense/relax/observe* the thighs.
◇ Point the toes and *tense/relax/observe* the legs.
◇ Flex the heels and *tense/relax/observe* the legs.
◇ *Tense/relax/observe* the abdominal area.
◇ *Tense/relax/observe* the buttocks.
◇ Press the shoulder blades into the mat, raising the chest, and *tense/relax/observe* the shoulder blades and chest.
◇ Curl the shoulders toward the ceiling and tuck the chin, and *tense/relax/observe* the upper back.
◇ Make the hands into fists and *tense/relax/observe* the hands.
◇ *Tense/relax/observe* the lower arms.
◇ *Tense/relax/observe* the upper arms.
◇ Flex wrists toward ceiling and *tense/relax/observe* arms and hands.
◇ Flex wrists toward floor and *tense/relax/observe* arms and hands.
◇ *Tense/relax/observe* shoulders.
◇ *Tense/relax/observe* neck.
◇ Open mouth wide, relax mouth.
◇ Scrunch face, knit eyebrows, *relax/observe* face.
◇ Scan the body for any tension and *tense/relax/observe* any area holding tension.
◇ Take six, slow diaphragmatic breaths, relaxing more deeply with each exhalation.
◇ Gently wiggle the fingers and toes.
◇ Rock the head gently from side to side.
◇ Bend the knees into the chest and clasp your hands around your shins and rock sideways several times.
◇ Come up into a sitting position. With your eyes still closed, experience how it feels to have your muscles relaxed. Open your eyes and observe the quiet of the room around you. Enjoy a minute of peace and tranquility. Then begin your activities.

**CONGRATULATIONS!**
You have now completed the first week's routine. Practice it or sections of it regularly and enjoy the benefits.

# REWARDING YOURSELF

AFTER A WEEK OF ADHERING to integrating the breathing, exercises, relaxation, and instant stress releasers into your day, give yourself a stress-reducing reward such as a massage, a long soak in the tub, or a walk in a nearby beautiful setting. Choose an appropriate bonus at the beginning of the week, and then reward yourself upon completion. The behavioral changes you are making (this week's physical exercises, the breathing technique, and the deep relaxation) and rewarding yourself are part of the behavioral approach in psychology. Rather than assuming the "impossible" task of deciphering the "black box" of the mind, behaviors are changed through goal setting and a specific course of action, followed by rewards (positive reinforcement) for completing the assigned task. This five-week stress management program is partially behavioral in approach because it helps you identify how you experience stress, the pragmatic techniques for change, and the reward system.

According to some behavioral therapists, rewarding a correct behavior elicits the desired change, while punishment (negative reinforcement) does not. Caring support and encouragement break a habit more successfully than criticism for getting off track. Focusing on positive change energizes continued change in the desired direction. If, however, you constantly confront an undesirable behavior or attitude, you usually end up more deeply enmeshed in the negative pattern.

Rather than an attempt to make you "less stressful," the program is a means for you to focus in the opposite direction; on techniques and behaviors that are relaxing. As you practice the techniques and appropriately reward yourself, less of your attention and energy are going into old stressful patterns, thus bringing you closer to your goal of being calm, yet full of vitality.

# WEEKLY REVIEW

## Lesson Summary

The foundation of stress management is proper breathing habits. Throughout the day consciously practice diaphragmatic breathing and correct posture to increase lung capacity and remove stale air. Calm your emotions by taking slow, deep *Diaphragmatic Breaths,* and visualize drawing peace in with the breath. To remember to practice, link your conscious breathing with an activity you perform several times a day, such as looking at your watch, washing your hands, or talking on the telephone.

THE CHART IN THE WEEKLY REVIEW at the end of each chapter relates practice of the relaxation skills to reducing your stress symptoms. Use the chart to map your progress for the week. Each week has a chart for you to complete. The purpose of the chart is to help you see the effect you can have on reducing the negative effects of stress. Use the chart to measure which coping skills alleviate stress for you. Do not feel guilty if you do not practice everything outlined every day.

## CHARTING YOUR PROGRESS

| RELAXATION SKILL | MON | TUES | WED | THUR | FRI | SAT | SUN |
|---|---|---|---|---|---|---|---|
| BREATHING EXERCISES | | | | | | | |
| PHYSICAL EXERCISES | | | | | | | |
| DEEP RELAXATION | | | | | | | |
| INSTANT STRESS RELEASER | | | | | | | |
| OTHER STRESS-REDUCING ACTIVITY (Jogging, listening to calming music, etc.) | | | | | | | |
| LEVEL OF STRESS (Rate on a scale of 1-10) | | | | | | | |

**Directions:** Place an X after each relaxation skill you practiced for that day. Evaluate your stress level at the end of each day on a scale of 1-10, with 10 representing a high level of stress. Review at the end of the week and note which techniques have been the most beneficial for you.

1) Standing Posture

2) Neck Rolls

3) Shoulder Shrugs

4) Palm Press

5) The Rag Doll

6) Chest Expander

7) The Cat (In Four Positions)

8) Seated Side Stretch

9) Spinal Twist on Back, Legs Crossed (In Two Positions)

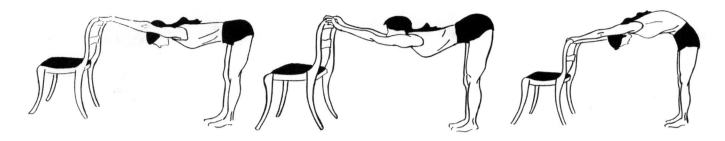

10) Full Body Stretch (In Three Positions)

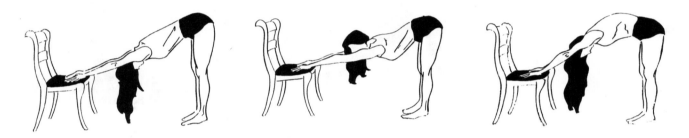

11) Advanced Full Body Stretch (In Three Positions)

12) Active Deep Relaxation (With Alternate Position)

WEEK TWO

# LESSON TWO: STRETCHING EXERCISES FOR STRESS REDUCTION

## How Muscles Work

All bodily movement, internal and external, is made possible by the muscular system. There are three types of muscles: the heart muscle; the smooth or internal muscles, which automatically regulate movement of the intestines, stomach, and blood vessels; and the skeletal muscles, which we consciously control for movement of the skeleton.

There are more than four hundred skeletal muscles. These muscles attach directly to the bone, or by means of a tendon, a cord of white fibrous tissue. Muscles are stretchy and elastic and are red in color due to their excellent blood supply. Tendons are not very elastic and have a relatively poor blood supply. Each muscle works like an elastic band. It contracts when it is working or tensed, and lengthens when it stops working and is relaxed.

Muscular movement aids circulation by squeezing blood and lymph through the vessels during exercise. Sluggish venous blood is squeezed out, allowing fresh blood in its place. After exercise a person feels energized because of the increased flow of oxygen to the body parts. Stretching aids circulation and reduces muscular tension. Elongation of the muscle fibers through stretching increases blood supply to the muscle and releases tension locked in muscles due to prolonged contraction. Overexertion or such emotions as fear, anxiety, resentment, or anger cause muscles to contract. Stretching relaxes the constricted muscle. For example, long hours at a desk coupled with the pressure of deadlines cause protracted tension in the neck and shoulders. The purpose of *The Fitness Option* exercises is to increase circulation and relax painful, contracted muscles through movement and stretching.

Four approaches to stretching are used in the program's exercises to release muscular tension: 1) static stretching, 2) contraction/relaxation, 3) the application of concentration, and 4) breathing techniques during the stretching action. These approaches are related to flexibility conditioning. Flexibility is defined by the range of motion through which you can move a joint. The ability of the ligaments, tendons, and muscles to elongate controls the range of motion of a joint.

## Static Stretching

One of the safest and most effective means of stretching a muscle is static stretching. The muscle is stretched to its limit (the *soft* side of pain) and held there for fifteen seconds up to a minute. When you stretch a muscle, it sends a message to the spinal cord reporting the muscle's elongated position. The nerves respond by causing a contraction reflex in the stretching muscle. The theory of static stretching is to hold the stretched position until this inhibiting resistance to the stretch is overridden by a second message. After holding a stretch for six seconds the tendon responds to the muscular tension and elongation by sending its own message to the spinal cord. The response is a relaxing reflex to protect the stretching muscle. By holding a stretched position, the initial contracting reflex is replaced with a relaxing reflex and the muscle further elongates. [12] This not only enhances flexibility but is excellent for stress management, because tense muscles are relaxed through this static stretching process.

## Stretching by Contracting/Relaxing

The second approach utilized in the program is "proprioceptive neuromuscular facilitation," a type of muscle strengthening exercise widely used by physical therapists. It is excellent for stretching tight muscles because it combines the practice of static stretching with alternating contraction and relaxation of opposing muscles. This enables muscles to work synergistically around a joint. As one muscle extends, the opposite muscle flexes. If you tense a muscle, there is a relax reflex response in the antagonistic muscle. [12] This knowledge is applied in the program's exercises to release tension held in the muscles due to stress. For example, tensing the abdominal muscles helps to release lower back tension.

## Enhanced Stretching Through Concentration

The benefits of the program's exercises are enhanced by practicing in a concentrated, slow, and quiet manner. Soothing background music may be used to help keep the movements fluid and the tempo relaxing. These exercises are not aerobic. Static stretching and slow movement encourage attention on the muscle being worked. This helps prevent overstretching and injury because the mind is attentive to how the stretch *feels*. If you hold a position and concentrate, you become aware of the amount and location of tension. This allows you to stretch safely and relax more deeply.

Concentration during the exercises helps quiet mental restlessness. Frequently, stress is created by worrying about a future possibility or a past mistake. The undisciplined mind jabbers constantly, repeating the same anxieties over and over again. The goal is to be able to shut out specific thoughts at will. Rather than dragging the ball and chain of worry into every activity, you can consciously choose to take mini-vacations from this voice. This will ultimately lead to clearer resolutions to your worries, because fresh perspectives and solutions often come from letting go for a while.

## Breathing in the Stretch

All of the exercises incorporate breathing techniques. The breath is used to aid in the stretching of a tense muscle and in quieting a restless mind. Specific breathing in the exercises changes a simple stretch into a stress reduction exercise for both physical and mental release of tension.

## Isolating Your Tension

It is useful to isolate the cause of your distress. Is the source of your tension physical, perhaps the result of sitting at a computer all day? The exercises will release such job-related tightness. Is your tension based on emotions stemming from an attitude or approach to life? Try sitting slumped down in your chair. Is this how you would sit if you were feeling joyful? Now sit with an uplifted chest and a smile on your face. Is this how you would sit if you were depressed? The body expresses our state of mind and how we are feeling. If you disguise a feeling, tension is created in the body in the act of suppressing the internal state.

Muscular tension due to emotional anxiety is released by stretching the tense area. Where do you hold your tension? Are your shoulder or neck muscles rigid due to worry? Do you find your lower jaw clenched with determination? Is your stomach in a knot as you cope with the day's pressures? Moving slowly and concentrating on the stretching muscle enables you to experience the difference between tension and relaxation. This knowledge helps you to relax tense muscles at will, not only in the exercises, but throughout the day.

Make an evaluation of yourself. Look in the mirror. Observe your posture and your facial expression. Do you see how you are physically expressing long-held attitudes? The exercises release these tensions and patterns in the short term and open avenues for new expression. They tangibly reduce physical, emotional, and mental stress.

**LOOK AT YOURSELF**
Look in the mirror. Observe your posture and your facial expression. Do you see how you are physically expressing long-held attitudes?

# INSTANT STRESS RELEASER

## Pinpointing Causes of Physical Tension

The purpose of this instant stress releaser is to begin the process of recognizing the relationship between your stress symptoms and the cause of those symptoms. From last week's instant stress releaser exercise you learned *how* you experience stress. This week, record the circumstances which *cause* your physical tension. Because of today's hectic pace, many of us have lost touch with bodily reactions. Look for the type of situations which cause you to clench your jaw, tense your stomach, or hunch your shoulders.

You may feel you are in a state of constant tension, that your back pain or headache is continual. Pain is never chronic in level of intensity. There are greater and lesser levels of tension. It may take special effort to pair a situation with an increase in your experienced stress. If you experience chronic tension or pain, jot down when there is greater intensity of pain.

Sometimes you may find causes that can be easily changed. If you wake up every morning with increased pain, the cause may be a faulty mattress or an incorrect sleeping position. Increased tension in the neck after a phone call may be related to the conversation itself or to how you are holding the phone. If your work keeps you on the phone constantly, change sides with each call. Constantly carrying a heavy purse over the same shoulder could be the cause of shoulder tension.

If the circumstances causing your tension cannot be changed, take three slow *Complete Breaths* (see below) before attending the important business meeting, before the upcoming interview, before you start your car engine. Make it a habit to quiet your mind and relax your body before and after stepping into difficult situations of any kind. Relax the body from head to toe on the exhalation of the first two *Complete Breaths,* and let the anxious thoughts go out with the exhalation of the third breath. Concentrate as you do the exercise.

Repeat the three *Complete Breaths* and physical and mental release after a crisis or difficult situation.

If you continue to practice the deep relaxation exercise each night as you go to sleep, it will become easier to instantly relax in a wave from head to toe during the exhalation of a *Complete Breath*.

**QUIET YOUR MIND**
Make it a habit to quiet your mind and relax your body before and after stepping into difficult situations of any kind.

# BREATHING EXERCISE

## Complete Breath

The *Complete Breath* is emotionally calming and physically energizing. With the *Complete Breath* one takes in approximately ten times more air than with normal breathing. It increases lung capacity and

clears the air passages. It uses all portions of the lungs: the lower, middle, and upper. Begin by relaxing the abdominal muscles to fill the lower lungs. Continue inhaling, expanding the ribcage sideways. Lastly, fill the upper portion of the lungs. Exhale in the reverse order: top to bottom. Think of filling a pitcher with water (the inhalation) and then emptying it (the exhalation).

To learn the *Complete Breath* correctly, begin by placing your palms at the sides of your ribs with your fingers coming around to the front. First exhale and squeeze the ribs from the sides (bringing the fingers of the two hands closer). Now inhale and try to push the hands apart. This exercise is designed to help you find the intercostal muscles between the ribs, and may take practice. Now remove your hands and fill the lungs slowly from bottom to top, taking two counts for each part, lower, middle, and upper. As you fill the upper portion, do not lift the shoulders. Feel a slight constriction in the throat. This constriction of the throat muscles tightening lifts the first rib up and out to allow more air into the upper lungs. Think of filling a balloon to help you expand the ribcage in back. To exhale, relax the throat, then contract in the ribcage area, and lastly contract the abdominal muscles completely.

Make the inhalation and the exhalation the same length of time. Count to two for each section: lower, middle, and upper, in the inhalation and the exhalation.

Breathe through your nose, but focus your attention at the throat and feel as if you are inhaling from there. To experience the difference between nostril breathing and throat breathing, first sniff using the nostrils and be aware of the sound; then slightly constrict the throat and inhale from there, the way you would if you were using a straw. You will notice the difference in sound when you breathe from the throat. Breathing from the throat expands the air passage in the throat, allowing in a greater supply of air. Make the inhalation one smooth, continuous flow followed by a smooth equal exhalation. Do not hurriedly take the next inhalation. Enjoy the stillness and relaxing release before taking the next inhalation.

**TO DO**
This week practice the *Complete Breath* each day to reduce your anxiety and increase your lung capacity.

# WEEK TWO ROUTINE

Diaphragmatic Breath

Marching in Place

Neck and Shoulder Arch and Curl

Standing Spinal Twist

Standing Side Stretch

On Back, Legs Up

Complete Breath

Lower Back Release

Inner Thigh Stretch

Twist on Back, Legs Parallel

Hamstring Stretch

Passive Deep Relaxation

ON THE FOLLOWING PAGES are illustrations and details of all the exercises for this week. First, read the instructions and practice all of the exercises once. As in *Week One*, use the At-A-Glance illustrations in the Weekly Review at the end of this chapter as a reminder of all of the exercises. During the week, integrate the exercises into your day if the ten minutes of exercises and ten minutes of deep relaxation are too time-consuming for you.

The following are guidelines on how to integrate this week's exercises into your day. It takes approximately three minutes to do the first five exercises: three *Diaphragmatic Breaths, Marching in Place,* a *Neck and Shoulder Arch and Curl,* a *Standing Side Stretch,* and a *Spinal Twist on Back, Legs Parallel.* When you first arise in the morning use them to wake up, take the kinks out, and stimulate circulation. Try the series again during the day to release tension. Experiment with placing your home phone in a location which allows you to relax on your back with your legs up the wall while in conversation. At the end of the day, the series against the wall relieves spinal tension, relaxes tired feet and legs, and releases mental fatigue. When you are watching television, turn off the sound during the advertising and practice a few of the stretches and the *Complete Breath.* Use the *Passive Deep Relaxation* to help quiet your body and mind before going to sleep.

# DETAILED INSTRUCTIONS ON WEEK TWO EXERCISES

### Diaphragmatic Breaths

Begin by standing and closing your eyes. Mentally scan your body from the feet upwards and make any adjustments needed for correct posture. With the eyes still closed, take three, slow *Diaphragmatic Breaths,* (see page 23). With the first exhalation, consciously relax your shoulders; with the second exhalation, relax your lower back and legs; during the third exhalation, mentally let your thoughts go out with the breath. Bring your attention into the present moment and focus on experiencing the releasing of tension in each exercise.

### Marching in Place

Vigorously march in place, lifting the knees toward the chest and staying on the toes. Swing the arms, with one arm coming forward towards the ceiling and the other arm behind you as high as it will go. March for half a minute, working towards a full minute by the end of the week.

Marching in Place

### Neck and Shoulder Arch and Curl

**First Position:** Remain in a standing position. While inhaling, turn your palms out and bring the arms straight out to the side and then over your head. While exhaling, interlock your fingers and roll your palms toward the ceiling. On the next inhalation, stretch through the arms toward the ceiling. To open the shoulders, as you exhale push your arms toward the back wall and pull down with your upper back muscles. Repeat for one more breath.

Neck and Shoulder Arch and Curl

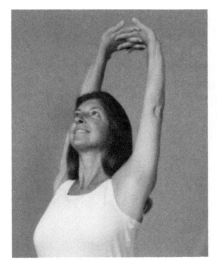

(First Position)

(Second Position)

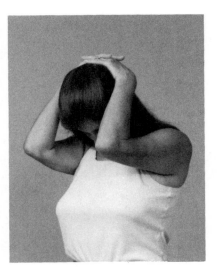

(Third Position)

**Second Position:** Bring your clasped hands to the back of your head. Arch your neck back with the elbows out to the side. Take three breaths in this position. To protect the lower back, tuck the pelvis and maintain gentle tension in the abdomen and buttocks. This is accomplished by tightening and lifting the abdominal muscles (shortening the space between the pubic bone and the ribs) while pulling down and tightening the buttocks muscles. If this is not clear to you, see discussion of *The Pelvic Tilt* in a lying down position in *Part III, Stress and Your Lower Back* (page 144).

As you hold the position, relax your neck and face and lift your chest. Lengthen through the back of the neck by pulling down with the upper back muscles.

**Third Position:** Bring the chin to the chest and take three more breaths. In this position, keep correct spinal posture by lifting the chest up to meet the chin. Do not hunch your shoulders; relax them.

Arch back for three more breaths. Next, inhale, raising your clasped hands, palms toward the ceiling, back into first position. As you exhale, lower your arms to your side.

Standing Spinal Twist

## Standing Spinal Twist

Separate your feet approximately one and one-half feet apart, with the toes pointing out. Bend your knees and place your hands, fingers pointing inward, on your thighs just above your knees. Let your upper body weight rest into your arms: Your shoulders will scrunch up by your ears. Keep a steady pressure on your hands to keep your knees out, over your toes. Push one shoulder forward across your body and down toward the carpet. Look behind you over the other shoulder. To increase the stretch, keep the lower back tucked, pulling your tailbone towards the carpet. Take three breaths in this position. Repeat to the other side. Return to the *Standing Position*. Gently shake each leg to release tension in the thighs.

Standing Side Stretch

## Standing Side Stretch

Stand with the feet approximately one and one-half feet apart. Place one hand below your hip, at the juncture of your hip and thigh. While inhaling, bring the other arm out to the side and then towards the ceiling. As you exhale, bend to the side. Hold for three breaths. With each inhalation stretch through the spine and upper arm. With each exhalation, relax deeper into the stretch. To protect the lower back, before bending to the side be sure to flatten the lower back by tilting the pelvis. Hold the lower body firm while in the side bend to experience a safe side stretch. Repeat the side stretch to the other side.

## On Back, Legs Up

Sit sideways next to the wall and then lean back and swing your legs up the wall, so that your buttocks are against the wall. If this is too much of a stretch for you, have your buttocks several inches away from the wall and the knees partially bent—or use the back of a chair, as shown in the photograph. Be sure to adjust to your flexibility level. If wall space is not available, use the back of a chair for this series of exercises. Bring your arms over your head on the floor with your palms toward the ceiling. To open the shoulders and chest, as you inhale, extend your arms and press them into the carpet. At the same time, stretch the back of your neck and your lower back by pushing them toward the floor (straightening the spine) and flex your heels toward the ceiling. As you exhale, relax your arms, spine, and legs. Repeat for three more breaths.

On Back, Legs Up

## Complete Breath

Remain on your back with your legs up the wall or against a chair. Bring your hands to your sides. Take three *Complete Breaths* while lying on your back with your legs up the wall for the routine practice. As discussed for this week's breathing exercise, begin by relaxing the abdominal muscles to fill the lower lungs. Continue inhaling, expanding the ribcage sideways. Lastly, fill the upper portion of the lungs. Exhale in the reverse order: top to bottom. Think of filling a pitcher with water (the inhalation) and then emptying it (the exhalation).

Complete Breath

## Lower Back Release

**First Position:** I experienced chronic lower back pain for six years and discovered this exercise the best one for relief of pain. While still lying on your back with your legs resting against a chair, or up the wall, bend your right knee into your chest and then turn the knee out to the side and rest your right ankle on the left thigh just above the left knee. If this is too much of a stretch for you, rest your right ankle against the chair or wall, next to the left thigh.

Lower Back Release (First Position)

(Second Position)

**Lower Back Release—Second Position:** Slowly bend the left knee. You will only need to move it a few inches to feel a stretch in the right buttock. Take six *Diaphragmatic Breaths* in this position, relaxing the stretching muscles as you exhale, increasing the bend in the left knee as the muscle relaxes. Repeat the exercise with the other leg.

Inner Thigh Stretch (Second Position)

Inner Thigh Stretch (First Position)

THE FOLLOWING THREE EXERCISES are excellent for increasing circulation in the lower back and stretching out muscles that connect into the lumbar spine.

### Inner Thigh Stretch

**First Position:** While remaining on your back, bend both knees to your chest with the soles of your feet against a wall or chair close to your buttocks (or hold them with your hands); then let the knees open out to the side. Place your hands (or elbows, if you are holding your feet with your hands) just above the knees and gently press the legs open. Take three *Diaphragmatic Breaths* in this position. Bring the knees together and straighten the legs up. You may prefer to practice this away from a wall or chair, as shown in this photograph.

**Second Position:** Open your legs out to the side with the legs straight, continuing to press with your hands. Take three breaths in this position. Use your hands to help bring the legs back together.

## Spinal Twist on Back, Legs Parallel

**First Position:** Remain on your back with your feet against the back of a chair, against the wall, or in the air as shown in this photograph. Bend your knees into your chest and take three *Diaphragmatic Breaths*, relaxing completely as you exhale.

**Second Position:** Bring your arms out to shoulder height on the carpet. Lower both legs to the left and turn your head in the opposite direction. Try to keep both shoulders on the carpet. To increase the stretch in the lower back, be sure to keep both knees as close to your chest as possible. Take three, slow *Complete Breaths* in this position. As you inhale, completely fill the chest and focus on the upper body stretch. Press your left elbow into the carpet to lift your chest and reposition; stretching through the right arm. As you exhale, concentrate on your lower body, relaxing your lower back, legs, and feet. Repeat to the other side.

## Hamstring Stretch

The following exercise is the safest position for protecting your lower back while stretching your hamstrings. Reduced flexibility of the hamstrings contributes to discomfort in the lower back.

**First Position:** Stretch out on your back. Bend both knees and place your feet on the floor with the heels close to the buttocks. Place a belt, strap, or towel around the sole of your right foot and start straightening your knee, but do not straighten it all the way.

**Second Position:** Keeping the buttocks on the floor and concentrating on the back of the thighs, gently pull on the strap, bringing the

Spinal Twist on Back, Legs Parallel (First Position)

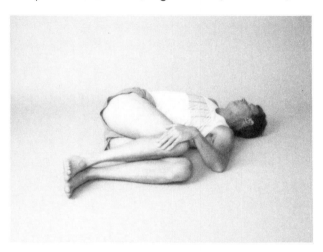

Spinal Twist on Back, Legs Parallel (Second Position)

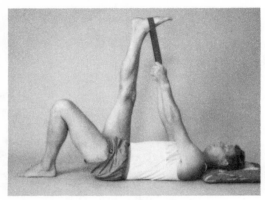

Hamstring Stretch (First Position)　　　Hamstring Stretch (Second Position)

"straight" leg closer to your face. Find the best position for your straight knee. If your hamstrings are tight, experiment with bending the straight leg until you are in a comfortable stretch. Keep the emphasis of the stretch in the middle of the back of the thigh rather than behind the knee. If you are able to keep the knee straight, be sure not to hyperextend it. Take six *Diaphragmatic Breaths* in this position, relaxing in the stretch during the exhalation. To stretch your calf, flex your heel towards the ceiling; to stretch hamstrings, point your toes towards the ceiling. Repeat to the other side.

## DEEP RELAXATION

LAST WEEK YOU LEARNED how to relax your muscles at will through actively tensing and relaxing them while you lay on your back. This week you will learn *Passive Deep Relaxation*. It is based on the yoga position *Savasana*, the corpse pose. Like a corpse, one lets go, not only of muscular tension, but also of emotional anxieties and mental restlessness. In my research and in classroom measurements I have repeatedly observed that ten-minute practice sessions result in a lowered metabolism and a calmed mind. Regular practice results in reduction of other stress symptomology.[9] According to B.K.S. Iyengar, yoga teacher and author of two classics in the field of hatha yoga, the corpse pose is considered the most beneficial of all the yogic exercises for stress management. He states that it relieves fatigue while simultaneously vitalizing the practitioner.[13] Variations of the corpse pose are taught in this program.

### Passive Deep Relaxation
**Phase One:** For *Passive Deep Relaxation*, stretch out on the carpet on your back with your legs stretched out or resting the calves on a chair, the way you did for *Active Deep Relaxation*. In *Passive Deep Relaxation* you focus your attention on each body part to become

aware of the sensations (possible tension) in the particular body part. Then you release the tension. You do not actively tense each body part before relaxing it as you did in *Active Deep Relaxation* last week. To enable the body to go into the relaxation response, the second phase consists of practicing a relaxing visualization for five minutes.

Stretch out on a carpet on your back, with your feet apart and the palms upward a foot or so away from your trunk. Close your eyes. Begin by taking a *Complete Breath*. Take a second *Complete Breath*, tensing gently on the inhalation and consciously relaxing on the exhalation. Take a third *Complete Breath*, lifting your head, arms, and legs several inches off the carpet and tensing as hard as you can on the inhalation, and releasing the head, arms, and legs down to the carpet on the exhalation. Then push the small of your back into the carpet while tensing the buttocks and the abdominal muscles. Follow this by pushing the shoulder blades into the carpet and lifting the chest slightly. Push the back of the neck gently toward the carpet, tucking the chin and pulling the shoulders towards your feet. Relax and make any adjustments you need to be comfortable. Place a pillow under your thighs or use a chair if your lower back is tense. This position straightens the lower back slightly, taking pressure off the intervertebral discs in the lumbar spine.

## Begin the relaxation process of each body part:

◇ Bring your attention down into the feet and become aware of how they feel; then consciously relax them.
◇ Now be attentive to the shins and calves, experiencing this part of yourself. Next, consciously let go of any residual tension there.
◇ Focus your mind on the thighs and be aware of the sensations there; then release more deeply.
◇ Observe the abdominal area and then soften there.
◇ Continue observing, experiencing, and relaxing each body part.
◇ *Observe/experience/relax* the buttocks.
◇ *Observe/experience/relax* the rib cage area.
◇ *Observe/experience/relax* the upper chest and upper back.
◇ *Observe/experience/relax* the shoulders.
◇ *Observe/experience/relax* the upper arms.
◇ *Observe/experience/relax* the lower arms.
◇ *Observe/experience/relax* the hands.
◇ *Observe/experience/relax* the neck and throat.
◇ *Observe/experience/relax* the tongue and inside the mouth.
◇ *Observe/experience/relax* each part of the face.
◇ *Observe/experience/relax* the scalp.

**Phase Two**: Spend five minutes quieting the mind. Use one of the following methods.

A. Play soft music during passive deep relaxation. After relaxing the body parts, focus on the music. If your mind wanders from the present moment, gently bring it back into the sound of the music. Anchor your mind to the present with the music. Do not try

**ENJOY A MINI-VACATION**
A ten-minute deep relaxation gives you the opportunity to let go of mental anxieties and physical tensions. Take three *Complete Breaths*: as you inhale, tense your muscles; as you exhale, relax them. Then consciously relax your muscles from your feet to your head. Next, for five minutes listen to soft, soothing music and/or visualize yourself relaxing in a grassy meadow; under a spreading oak tree; or on a warm, sandy, beach.

to listen; *allow* yourself to listen. Trying or willing the mind into the present will raise your blood pressure. Instead, observe when your mind has wandered, and, without guilt or disappointment in yourself, bring your attention back to the sound. Listen to the notes, the sounds, and the pauses without analyzing them. Use music that is peaceful and calming.

B. Continue to scan the body for tension and relax wherever you find any tension. If your have an area that is chronically sore, focus your attention there and take a minute experiencing the sensations there. Mentally document the tingling, pressure, warmth, or other sensations you are feeling. You will notice that the pain lessens as much as half if you discard the label "pain," and without judgment or avoidance, experience the sensations of the traumatized area.

C. Choose an affirmation, poem, or inspiring quote and repeat it to yourself or record it on a tape. Sri Kriyananda, author of numerous books on yoga, including one on yoga postures, uses the following affirmation. Repeat it slowly to yourself, and experience its meaning. "Bones, muscles, movement I surrender now; anxiety, elation and depression, churning thoughts—all these I give into the hands of peace."[14] My affirmation is, "Peace within brings peace without."

D. Create a visualization which you can use mentally or pre-record. For a theme take a form in nature and focus on it. For example, visualize yourself at the beach stretched out on the warm sand, listening to the sound of the waves and watching a bird soar above you in the crystal blue sky. Or perhaps see yourself sitting beside a tumbling, crashing waterfall, watching the water cascade over the cliff into a deep, dark pool beneath. Breathe in the cool, moist air, and let the beauty around you regenerate and relax you. Or you may see yourself in the quiet solitude of the desert watching the yellow, orange, and red of a sunset change to soft lavenders and grays.

Take a complete breath and gently wiggle your fingers and toes. Bring your knees to your chest and rock side to side, and then come into a sitting position. With your eyes still closed, observe the effects of stretching and consciously relaxing. After opening your eyes, take a minute to be still, remaining in the quiet attitude of the relaxation exercise.

## *REWARDING YOURSELF*

POSITIVELY REINFORCE YOURSELF for keeping up with the breathing and exercises. What is it that you would like to do or enjoy that you have not permitted yourself in a while? If you did not get to all of the relaxation skills this week, that is o.k.; just keep your attention on what you are doing to make changes, and congratulate and reward yourself.

# WEEKLY REVIEW

## Lesson Summary

Stretching is a stress management tool for releasing accumulated physical and emotional tension in your body. As you stretch, breathe consciously, holding the stretched position for half-a-minute. Relax more deeply into the stretch with each exhalation. If you have a sedentary job, practice the neck and shoulder exercises as often as possible.

## CHARTING YOUR PROGRESS

| MON | TUES | WED | THUR | FRI | SAT | SUN | RELAXATION SKILL |
|---|---|---|---|---|---|---|---|
| □ | □ | □ | □ | □ | □ | □ | BREATHING EXERCISES |
| □ | □ | □ | □ | □ | □ | □ | PHYSICAL EXERCISES |
| □ | □ | □ | □ | □ | □ | □ | DEEP RELAXATION |
| □ | □ | □ | □ | □ | □ | □ | INSTANT STRESS RELEASER |
| □ | □ | □ | □ | □ | □ | □ | OTHER STRESS-REDUCING ACTIVITY (Jogging, listening to calming music, etc.) |
| □ | □ | □ | □ | □ | □ | □ | LEVEL OF STRESS (Rate on a scale of 1-10) |

**Directions:** Place an X after each relaxation skill you practiced for that day. Evaluate your stress level at the end of each day on a scale of 1-10, with 10 representing a high level of stress. Review at the end of the week and note which techniques have been the most beneficial for you.

1) Marching in Place

2) Neck and Shoulder Arch and Curl
(First and Second Position)

2) Neck and Shoulder
Arch and Curl (Third Position)

3) Standing Spinal Twist

4) Standing Side Stretch

5) On Back, Legs Up

6) Complete Breath

8) Inner Thigh Stretch
(First Position)

7) Lower Back Release (In Two Positions)

8) Inner Thigh Stretch (Second Position)

9) Spinal Twist on Back, Legs Parallel
(In Two Positions)

10) Hamstring Stretch (In Two Positions)

11) Passive Deep Relaxation (With Alternate Position)

WEEK THREE

## LESSON THREE: QUIET TIME AND MEDITATION FOR STRESS MANAGEMENT

### Quiet Time

Each one of us has become a juggler; balancing work, duties, responsibilities, recreation time, family commitments, and friends. We are always adding one more dazzle, one more fret. We have become perfectionists in the art of cramming more and more into already full schedules.

Unlike the juggler, we do not walk away from our performances. We have not left time for ourselves. We have no quiet time for recharging our batteries. We allow no breather from the pressures of deadlines, sales quotas, traffic jams, exams, relationships, and mental turmoil. For our mental health and physical well-being each of us needs a respite from the flurry of activity, constant external pressures, and our own clamoring thoughts.

Quiet time is that break. It is a pause for psychological and mental release, and a recess to calm oneself. Traditionally this has meant meditation, a proven technique for achieving the relaxation response.[7,8] It is included in the program because of its benefits in stress reduction. Explore the other ways of experiencing quiet time given in the program if you do not have the time or inclination to practice meditation. Like meditation, the personal quiet time techniques increase your ability to control your thought processes. For example, you might walk or sit in solitude, consciously experiencing a breeze across your bare skin, the sights and smells of nature around you, or the feel of the earth beneath your feet. Sitting or walking with your attention in the experience of the moment, shedding thoughts of the past or future, gives you a healing breather in your day. Allow time to *be* rather than to *do*. We are so busy doing, we miss the beauty of being, experiencing what and who we are. See *Week Five* for a list of creative adaptations of personal quiet time.

The essence of quiet time/meditation is to empty the mind of the persistent noise of nagging thoughts. By clearing away the

**TIME**
Allow time to *be* rather than to *do*. We are so busy doing, we miss the beauty of being, experiencing what and who we are.

thoughts, you come in contact with silence. You experience awareness of the field that thoughts occupy and over-whelm. Meditation and creative quiet time are tools used to remove the objects (thoughts) from your field of consciousness. They are a means to remove the habitual thought patterns and perceptions with which we frame our lives. This does not mean you lose your perspective; rather, by going into the field of quiet you can reform your ideas and expand your limited view. Most importantly, you can discover and enjoy this serene, peaceful part of yourself.

## Meditation Defined

Meditation is defined as the act of sitting in a quiet setting, usually with closed eyes, focusing on an object such as the breath, a sound, or a word. Metaphorically speaking, picture yourself stretched out in a grassy green meadow. In your hand you hold the strings to colorful, bouncing helium balloons. These red, yellow, blue, and green balloons block your vision of the clear, blue sky of your mind. As you relax and quiet yourself, release the strings of your balloon-packaged thoughts until the sky of your mind is clear and emptied of thoughts. The focus is narrowed to one particular thought (balloon) until all the other thoughts dissolve and recede. The final step is to release that remaining thought and experience the sky (pure awareness). A definition that is useful and covers the spectrum of various types of meditation states that "meditation refers to a family of techniques which have in common a conscious attempt to focus attention in a non-analytical way and an attempt not to dwell on discursive, ruminating thought."[15] Patanjali, who codified yoga, defined meditation as the "controlling of the thought waves of the mind."[16]

Although there are many forms of meditation, it is considered an exact science with only superficial differences. All methods transform the mind from its restless state to one of equilibrium, going through specific stages to reach this equilibrium. At the first stage, one becomes aware of the restlessness and chaos of the mind. Secondarily, one discovers the associative train of thoughts, and thirdly, one learns to dismiss the thoughts rather than become involved in them. Over time, according to this progression, the mind and body are calmed and the inherent state of peace and joy is experienced. Thus, meditation provides a reference point, a center from which one's actions can derive stability and direction.[17]

## Therapeutic Value of Meditation

The practice of meditation does not necessarily involve a particular dogma or religion and can be used as a discipline for stress management without the involvement of rituals or belief systems. Many Western health practitioners recommend meditation for its therapeutic value. In his book *Mind As Healer, Mind As Slayer*, Kenneth Pelletier states that meditation is excellent for stress

**MEDITATION IS NOT A RELIGION**
The practice of meditation does not necessarily involve a particular dogma or religion and can be used as a discipline for stress management without the involvement of rituals or belief systems.

reduction, because it "breaks into the degenerative syndrome of prolonged stress reactivity very effectively."[18] He points out that meditation fosters an attitude of detached introspection of one's self and one's relationship to the world, consequently promoting positive life changes.

Other researchers support Pelletier's position, stating that meditation changes the way an individual reacts to stress.[17,19] The practice of meditation promotes control over one's life situation, creates an increased sense of self-regard, and develops a sense of inner personal strength and balance. Each of these results helps in the management of stress.[20] According to Selye, meditation and stress are mirror opposites. Meditation moves a person away from the wear and tear of stress. Meditation gives a "complete rest" which allows the body to "forget" somatic reactions to stress.[21]

Researchers agree that meditation elicits the relaxation response and that the brain wave pattern during meditation shows an increase in alpha activity, which is associated with calmness. However, there is disagreement as to whether or not meditation in and of itself is enough to effect a cure for anxiety. A number of researchers state that treatment for anxiety is most effective when meditation is part of a holistic program including exercise, deep relaxation, and personalized counseling.[19,22,23,24] This book is an example of such a holistic approach.

## How To Meditate

*The R-E-L-A-X-ation Meditation* taught this week under "Deep Relaxation" is specifically for stress management. Also experience the meditations taught in *Week Four* and *Week Five* under "Deep Relaxation." All three meditations elicit the relaxation response if practiced correctly, and can result in release from a multitude of stress symptomologies if practiced regularly.

General rules for meditation are:

1. Maintain a comfortable position so that you are not distracted by bodily discomfort.

2. Let the mind remain passive rather than straining or trying to concentrate.

3. Be in a quiet environment. If this is difficult, use soft, sponge ear plugs. Unplug the telephone for uninterrupted quiet.

4. Choose an object for one-pointed concentration, such as your breath; a word or phrase; a short, inspiring quote; or an uplifting quality.

5. Practice in the same place, at the same time each day, to enhance your practice.

## Changing Negative Thought Patterns

There is a direct link between the habitual internal and external language a person uses and the resulting emotional and physical health of the individual. In meditation one observes the power of

**MEDITATION**
The practice of meditation promotes control over one's life situation, creates an increased sense of self-regard, and develops a sense of inner personal strength and balance.

**WEEDING OUT NEGATIVE THOUGHTS**
Meditation is an excellent tool for discovering negative habitual patterns of thought.

thoughts, their ability to govern moods and behavior, and their vital role in health and healing. Meditation is an excellent tool for discovering negative habitual patterns of thought. Attitudes, beliefs, and values underlying the labels one uses come under scrutiny, and once discovered, these unhealthy patterns of limitation and negation can be changed.

"If you change your mind you change the world" is a Zen Buddhist saying which asserts that it is our perception of reality that actually molds our reality. We choose to see only what fits with our view or interests. Concurring, cognitive psychotherapists state that it is our thoughts that control our emotions which, in turn, create our behavior. In this chain of events we need not focus on changing our mood or changing our behavior. Instead, they will naturally change as our perspective on ourselves and on the world around us changes. The practice of meditation trains us to be able to change our minds, to choose our thoughts rather than becoming a victim of them. By gaining entrance into the thought process, we can positively alter our moods and behavior.

Meditation also broadens one's horizons by expanding awareness beyond personal thought patterns and perspectives. Life, along with the stressors it fosters, is full of ambiguities, and sometimes we need to see life from a perspective different from our own limited one. The act of quieting the mental tape allows an opening for expanded vistas. It lifts one out of a prejudicial viewpoint and into a more objective view of a given situation.

## Meditation: Questions and Answers

The practice of meditation leads to many questions. This section answers those which are often asked in my classes. These answers are based on personal practice of meditation for over twenty years and from the wisdom obtained from other meditators and researchers. Hopefully, the following will answer questions that arise from your practice. You may want to first practice the meditation given in this week's "Deep Relaxation" before reading these questions and answers.

## Why do I tend to fall asleep when I practice meditation?

In practicing meditation we are attempting to come into a state of quiet awareness. It is much like trying to still the swings of a pendulum. Our minds are either restless and full of activity as we attempt to meditate, or we tend to fall asleep. Our minds resist the discipline by unruly continuation of a constant stream of thoughts, or escape the discipline by drifting into sleep. Realize that this is a natural resistance and then try some of the following suggestions. Sit, rather than lying in the relaxation position. If you are already sitting, sit away from the back of the chair with an erect spine. If you are still sleepy, inhale and tense the whole body then allow it to relax, or stand up and stretch before continuing with your practice.

Also, do not think of meditation as something boring. Pay more attention to the detail of the experience and it becomes fascinating; you will not fall asleep because it is so interesting! If the object of your concentration is your breath, have you noticed the difference in temperature between the incoming and outgoing breath? Have you experienced the pause between the exhalation and the inhalation? Have you felt the sense of the universe exhaling into you as you inhale, and inhaling as you exhale? Have you felt your muscles become heavy and warm as you relax more deeply? Have you begun to experience the meaning of the word that you are repeating? You are practicing the art of concentration, of staying in the present, focused on a single object. Training the mind to concentrate is a most difficult, yet rewarding, discipline.

### Why does my mind become so restless when I sit to meditate?

Your mind does not become restless when you sit to meditate. In the attempt to quiet it, you become aware of its restless commotion. In the first stage of meditation one becomes aware of the chaos of the mind: the repetition of thoughts, the skipping from subject to subject, the fleeting thoughts, and the conflicting thoughts. The restlessness has not increased; you are now aware of it.

### Why do I sometimes feel depressed or angry during deep relaxation/meditation?

Meditation allows access to our subconscious. As we continue to practice, we relax the barrier between conscious and subconscious thoughts. If we have had a previous negative experience, sometimes we repress that experience to avoid the pain that memory has for us. By relaxing the barrier, the past memory "bubbles up" to surface awareness, and we feel the emotion of that experience. Meditation offers us the opportunity to reassess a negative, stressful experience, and to accept its pain and lessons. Since we are in a calm state of mind and more objective than in our normal state, the event can be seen in a new light.

**GAINING PERSPECTIVE**
Meditation offers us the opportunity to reassess a negative, stressful experience, and to accept its pain and lessons.

### How long should I meditate?

In this five-week program, ten minutes a session is allotted for deep relaxation/meditation. This is a sufficient amount of time to reap the benefits of reduced stress symptomology. Dr. Herbert Benson, researcher and author of two books on meditation, recommends meditating once daily for ten to twenty minutes. Several spiritual traditions recommend meditating twice daily for ten to twenty minutes. The point is that if you make an effort every day, it begins to influence you outside of the practice. You are calmer in your interactions in life and often are more "solution oriented," rather than "problem oriented." Meditate regularly, often enough and long enough for it to have an impact. I recommend meditating twice daily for ten minutes to effect changes in your stress symptoms. Personally, I do not time my meditations. I keep the meditation short enough to end with a sense of enjoyment of the experience of meditation, yet long enough for my mind to quiet. If I keep having thoughts, I say to myself, "All right, fine, you just babble on, but I will not get up from sitting until there has been a quiet time also."

### How do I choose a word or phrase to concentrate on during meditation?

Choose a word or phrase which is calming or inspirational for you. It can have spiritual significance, be an ideal, or simply be a neutral term such as "one." All of these forms elicit the relaxation response. The essence of many meditation techniques, including Dr. Benson's technique, is the one-pointed focus harmonized with the exhalation. Using a meaningful word or phrase introduces the "faith factor" and has results befitting that faith. Once you choose a phrase or quality, do not keep changing it. The effect comes from the repeated concentration on, and experience of, the word or phrase. If you have chosen "one," you will derive the benefits of repeated experience of the relaxation response. Using the word "one," Dr. Benson has had significant results in reducing high blood pressure. By introducing the "faith factor," his patients have had reduction in other symptoms of stress such as backaches, migraine headaches, and insomnia. [8]

It is said you become that upon which you meditate. In my own experience and in talking with numerous students and clients over the years, this statement holds true. If you say "relax" on every exhalation in your practice, you become more relaxed outside your practice. If you practice *The R-E-L-A-X-ation Meditation* given this week under "Deep Relaxation," you will experience more peace in your life. You will be able to consciously keep your muscles relaxed, and your state of mind will be more peaceful through the regular practice of this meditation. Your focus is peace, thus you become more peaceful. If your focus is joy or love or courage, you begin to express those qualities in your daily life.

### I seem to get more out of the *Active Deep Relaxation* technique. What am I doing wrong in the other forms of deep relaxation?

You are not doing anything wrong. If you find yourself resisting the *Passive* and *Meditative Deep Relaxations,* do the *Active Deep Relaxation* of tensing and relaxing each of the body parts. This form of deep relaxation is excellent for releasing residual tension in the muscles.

**MEDITATION AND STRESS**
Researchers have successfully used meditation to reduce such stress symptoms as backaches, migraine headaches, and insomnia.

## Does the technique of meditation work even if I do not believe in it?

Yes, it does. *The R-E-L-A-X-ation Meditation* and the other deep relaxation techniques elicit the relaxation response and an alpha brain wave pattern whether or not there is belief in the technique. It is rather like the jogger who runs because his doctor tells him it is good for him, not because he believes in it. Deep relaxation and meditation, like jogging, work whether or not there is faith in the practice.

## I have never meditated before. How do I know the long-term effects are not harmful?

In all the research available, including research on people who have meditated a long time, there is no evidence of its having a negative effect. There are situations when a person should not meditate, however. If you are in a state of depression, do not meditate. When you are depressed, peace and calmness are subtly too similar to depression. Meditation might only intensify your depression. Rather than meditating when you are experiencing depression, choose an activity to raise your level of energy. Try some of the exercises; get yourself moving. It has been found that a mood-elevating hormone is released in the brain through exercise. Jog if you feel up to it, but if not, do the program's exercise and active deep relaxation. Or go for a walk. Getting outside and walking briskly also has an uplifting effect. Walk focusing on the present, not dwelling on the cause of your depression. One symptom of stress is depression. If these suggestions do not help, I recommend your seeing a physician. A possible cause could be a nutritional deficiency, or you may need the professional support and guidance of a counselor.

A psychotic individual should not meditate. If you are under psychiatric care, consult with your doctor before meditating. Meditation increases awareness of subtle aspects of yourself. If your personality structure is weak or your past too difficult to look at, your natural defense mechanisms are protecting you. In a clinical setting, a psychotherapist helps you in the process of getting in touch with yourself.

**IS MEDITATION ALWAYS BENEFICIAL?**
In most situations meditation is highly beneficial, but if you are deeply depressed, rather than meditating, choose an activity such as walking to raise your level of energy, or seek the guidance of a counselor.

## Does deep relaxation/meditation kill ambition?

No, it does not. It allows insight and clarification of priorities through expansion of awareness. It does not kill energy and enthusiasm. It is a motivating factor for active involvement in life. Deep relaxation/ meditation calms restlessness, releases emotional tension stored in the body, and frees the energy used to suppress past events.

**Doesn't success often come from focusing on a problem until a solution becomes evident? Your suggestion of mini-vacations from thought may result in losing a creative idea.**

Successful business people and those of great genius have developed the skill of concentration. Creative inspiration does take a laser-like focus on the "problem" at hand. In fact, two requisites for meditation are concentration on a single concept/object and being in the present moment. In this sense these people are practicing a form of meditation. (See "Creative Quiet Time" in *Week Five* for more quiet time examples.)

As long as the subject of concentration is your choice of focus, it is not stressful. Innovators often hold an idea in the back of their minds while engaged in other activities, but this is by choice. It is when the focus cannot be dropped from the mind at will that it becomes a condition for stress. The program's techniques place emphasis on the practice of keeping the mind in the present. The object is to gain control over your mind. Once you have developed the ability to choose what you think about, you can focus on a topic as long as you want to do so. The mini-vacation concept is the idea of taking a break before coming at it again from a refreshed and calm perspective.

**CALMING THE "CROSS-CURRENTS"**
All too often we work at cross-purposes with ourselves. The quiet of meditation highlights those inconsistencies.

**I have read that meditation is used as a tool for success in sports, business, and creative endeavors. How is this possible?**

Since meditation is, in part, training in the art of concentration, that skill can then be beneficially used in business, sports, or creative thinking to real advantage. It is the inability to stay with a subject, the fleeting, distracting thoughts, that result in mediocrity.

The quiet of meditation also allows one to remember the longer rhythms of life, to look beyond the short-term goals. This helps you to prioritize your goals and match those goals appropriately with allocations of your time. It clarifies where the "thwarting cross currents" are in your life and how to bring those currents into a supportive flow of your long-term goals. All too often we work at cross-purposes with ourselves. The quiet of meditation highlights those inconsistencies. Success in any field is enhanced by such prioritization.

Because deep relaxation and meditation elicit the relaxation response, they result in a calmer, more confident you. Approaching any endeavor from an anxious state reduces effectiveness. We think and act more efficiently when we are calm and relaxed. Meditation and the other techniques are training for you to be able to experience the difference between being tense or relaxed and then being able to choose to be relaxed, either mentally or physically.

# INSTANT STRESS RELEASER

## Concentration on the Present

1.   Continue practicing the instant stress releasers from *Weeks One* and *Two*. The assignment for this week is training in managing your thinking patterns. The inability to stop the torrent of thoughts can be a downfall in stress management. Do you have mental tapes that continue to play repeatedly?

Expand your practice of concentration during the physical exercises, breathing, and relaxation into your daily activities. The skill of holding the mind in the present is an excellent tool in stress reduction. Choose an activity that you do regularly, such as walking from your car to the office, brushing your teeth, or doing the dishes.

Rather than letting the mind wander or worry, use the time to train your mind to be attentive to the activity at hand. Observe the detail of your body's movement or focus on the sights and sounds around you. Witness the movement of thoughts into the past or future, and without self-criticism, pull the attention back into the present activity.

This assignment will help you gain the ability to choose what you think about and when you think about it. Strategizing, organizing, and ruminating are all natural and beneficial, but during the assignment let go of these mental activities. Each day choose a new activity in which to practice being in the present moment.

2. Also practice the following stress releaser this week:  Use the *Three-Part Rhythmic Breath* to rapidly calm yourself. Take six breaths—inhaling, holding the breath, and exhaling—to the count of ten, counting backwards on the exhalation. Do this any time you feel mounting pressure and anxiety. This technique is used across the country in hospitals and in stress management clinics and classes for reducing anxiety.

# BREATHING EXERCISE

## Three-Part Rhythmic Breath

The *Three-Part Rhythmic Breath* has a calming effect both mentally and physically. It consists of inhaling, holding the breath, and then exhaling. Each part is of equal length. Inhale and exhale the way you have learned with the complete breath: Inhale, filling the lower, middle, and then upper lungs, and exhale, emptying upper, middle, and then lower lungs. While you hold your breath between the inhalation and the exhalation, relax your shoulders and your face. Maintain correct posture throughout the exercise. Count to ten as you inhale. Hold the breath for ten counts. As you exhale, count from ten back down to one. Use a count comfortable for you, keeping the rhythm the same for inhaling, holding the breath, and exhaling. Practice five more times and feel the calming effects.

# WEEK THREE ROUTINE

Complete Breath
Three-Part Rhythmic Breath
Sitting Spinal Stretches
The Rope Climb
Shoulder and Chest Stretch
Straight Arm Rotations
Standing Forward Bend
Spinal Twist on Back, One Leg Bent
The R-E-L-A-X-ation Meditation

**BE CREATIVE!**
Continue being creative with your stretching and breathing. What are you doing while waiting for appointments, in grocery and bank lines, in traffic jams, or on hold on the telephone?

FIRST, READ AND PRACTICE all of the exercises once. Once you are familiar with these exercises, use them exclusively, or continue using some of the exercises from *Week One* and *Week Two* in combination with the exercises from this week's routine. Each week the routines include exercises for releasing tension in the neck, shoulders, spine, and legs, so be sure to include exercises that focus on each area. Bend the spine forward, backward, to each side, and then twisting left and right.

Continue being creative with your stretching and breathing. What are you doing while waiting for appointments, in grocery and bank lines, in traffic jams, or on hold on the telephone? Rather than *becoming* impatient and frustrated, use the time to practice the *Complete Breath, Diaphragmatic Breath,* or *Three-Part Rhythmic Breath* taught this week. Think of this time as an opportunity to quiet and calm yourself, a built-in stress break in the midst of a hectic schedule. Approach waiting with this perspective to create an instant stress releaser for yourself.

The sitting spinal stretches given this week can be adapted to a chair. Relax, bending forward, and let your head go towards the floor; arch back, pushing into the seat of the chair with your hands, or doing the *Chest Expander;* bend to each side; twist to the left and then right, pushing your hand against the outside of the opposite thigh to increase the rotation. Alternate these stretches with *The Rope Climb* and any of the neck and shoulder exercises. Never sit for long periods without stretching or getting up and walking. Take short stress breaks to stimulate circulation, release tension, and clear the mind.

Taking frequent, one-minute stress breaks is beneficial to your health and your peace of mind. Once you choose an exercise, associate it with a time and activity to help reinforce practice.

# DETAILED INSTRUCTIONS ON WEEK THREE EXERCISES

## Complete Breath

Begin this week's routine by sitting comfortably on the carpet with your eyes closed. Sit on the edge of a pillow to help maintain correct posture in the lumbar spine. Take three *Complete Breaths.* Use the time during the three slow breaths to let go of tensions. Draw your attention into the present moment by concentrating on your breath and consciously relaxing. Feel yourself let go more deeply with each exhalation. Play soft, calming music to aid you in this relaxing process.

## Three-Part Rhythmic Breath

Practice six rounds of the *Three-Part Rhythmic Breath,* inhaling, holding the breath, and exhaling to equal counts. Upon completion, observe the effects of the *Complete Breath* and the *Three-Part Rhythmic Breath.* You may prefer to do both of these breathing exercises lying down on your back.

Sitting Spinal Stretches (First Position)

## Sitting Spinal Stretches

**First Position:** While sitting in a cross-legged position, inhale and lift up through the spine. As you exhale, bend forward from the hips with your hands on the floor in front of you. Remember to keep the spine in correct posture as you bend forward. This is more important than getting your head to the floor. Reach through the arms and relax in your hips. Take four *Diaphragmatic Breaths* in this position. On the next inhalation come back into the original sitting position.

Sitting Spinal Stretches (Second Position)

    **Second Position:** Place your hands behind you, in line with your shoulders. Begin arching your chest, keeping your chin tucked to your chest. Lift up onto your knees and tighten your buttocks. Let the head arch back, if it is comfortable for you. Keep the buttocks tight and the chest lifted and press evenly into your hands. Take four *Diaphragmatic Breaths* in this position. On the last exhalation come back to the original sitting position.

    **Third Position:** For a side stretch, begin by placing your left hand on the floor. As taught in *Week One,* inhale and bring the right arm out to the

Sitting Spinal Stretches (Third Position)

side and then over your head, stretching toward the ceiling. As you exhale, begin bending to the left. With each inhalation reach further with the right arm and be sure to keep the chest open, as in correct standing posture. With each exhalation, relax further into the stretch. By the second or third breath you may have relaxed to the side far enough to have your left forearm on the floor. Keep both buttocks on the mat. Think of the hip on the stretching arm side as the point from which to stretch. From the sitting up position to the full stretch use six *Diaphragmatic Breaths*. Inhale and come up out of the position with the right arm reaching toward the ceiling. As you exhale, lower your right arm back down to your side. Repeat the stretch with the left arm.

The Rope Climb

### The Rope Climb
From a standing position, bring both arms over your head and start climbing an imaginary rope. As you climb, come up on your toes and stretch up first with one hand and then with the other hand. Feel the stretch from the hips by leaning slightly to each side. Stretch six times on each side.

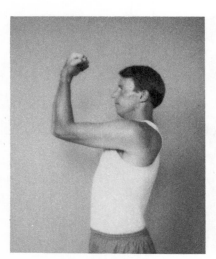

Shoulder and Chest Stretch
(First Position)

Shoulder and Chest Stretch
(Second Position)

Shoulder and Chest Stretch
(Advanced Position)

### Shoulder and Chest Stretch
**First Position:** While standing, bring both arms together in front of you at shoulder height with the elbows bent ninety degrees. Make the hands into fists with the palms facing toward you and relax your shoulders. Focus your attention on your upper back and shoulder area and lift the elbows slightly. Keeping your attention on the same area, push your fists away from you an inch at a time, until you feel the stretch in the scapular area (shoulder blades). In this stretched position take three *Diaphragmatic Breaths*.

**Second Position:** Open the arms out to the side, expanding the chest. While taking three breaths in this position, be sure to keep the elbows shoulder height and the shoulders pulled down so that your neck is not scrunched. Repeat the whole exercise, including the first and second positions, two more times.

**Advanced Position:** To increase the stretch of the scapular area in the first position: Cross one elbow over the other one and wrap the wrists around each other so that the palms can press into each other. Notice the increase in the stretch when you slightly lift the elbows and push both hands an inch further from your face. Keep the shoulders relaxed down. Take three *Diaphragmatic Breaths* in this position, and then open into the second position for three breaths. Close back into the advanced version with the other elbow on top, and take three breaths. Repeat the cycle once more, alternating elbows.

## Straight Arm Rotations

Extend your arms straight out to the side at shoulder height with your palms facing forward, and then lift the arms slightly back and up. While keeping your arms stiff with tension in the muscles and pushing the shoulder blades toward the spine, rotate in small (three-inch) circles six times. Relax your arms to the side briefly and then repeat six rotations in the opposite direction.

Straight Arm Rotations

## Standing Forward Bend

**First Position:** Spread the feet apart a bit wider than your shoulders and stand slightly pigeon-toed. Clasp your hands behind your back. As you inhale, lift the chest and extend the spine. As you exhale, bend forward from the hips, keeping the spine in correct alignment. Once you are as far over as you can go without straining, bring the clasped arms over your head. If the stretch feels strained behind your knees, or you cannot maintain the spine in correct alignment, bend your knees slightly.

This is a wonderful stretch for the shoulders, hips, and hamstrings. Hold the stretched position for six breaths. To come out of the position, bring the hands back to the buttocks, bend the knees, and come up with a curled spine. Or, if your lower back is strong, come up with a straight spine the same way you went into the stretch. Briefly keep the chin tucked when you reach the standing position to slow down the return of blood from your head.

If it is hard to keep your spine straight, continue practicing the *Full Body Stretch* given in *Week One,* in which you place your hands on a chair for the stretch.

**Second Position:** If the first position is a comfortable stretch for you, stand with your feet together in correct, erect posture. Exhale,

Standing Forward Bend (First Position)

Standing Forward Bend
(Second Position)

bending from the hips with a flat back and hands sliding down the backs of your legs. Clasp your ankles from behind. As you inhale, press into your heels and push your buttocks towards the ceiling. As you exhale, rather than bringing your face towards your knees, release tension in the neck and stretch the spine by extending the top of your head towards the floor.

If you cannot go down this far, use your arms as a brace by placing your hands on your thighs or shins with the elbows straight. Lift your chest away from your body and keep the back flat (as you did while using a chair).

Do *The Rag Doll* (page 28) if this exercise is too difficult, or if you get more benefit from relaxing away tension rather than stretching it out.

## Spinal Twist on Back, One Leg Bent

**First Position:** Lie down on your back with both arms straight out to the side at shoulder height. Place your right foot beside your left knee and then shift your hips two inches toward your right foot. Now place your right foot on your leg just above your knee. Keeping both shoulders on the carpet, slowly lower your right knee toward the carpet on the left side of your body. Take three breaths in this position.

**Second Position:** To increase the rotation of the spine, place your left hand on your right leg just above your knee and gently press the knee toward the carpet. At the same time pull the knee an inch or more toward your left shoulder. You will feel this stretch in the lower back, the chest, and the upper back. Keep stretching through the straight leg and pressing the right shoulder toward the floor. This is more important than getting the knee to the floor. To help hold the shoulders down, press the left elbow into the carpet to lift

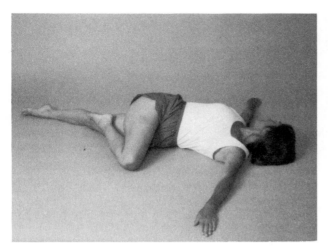

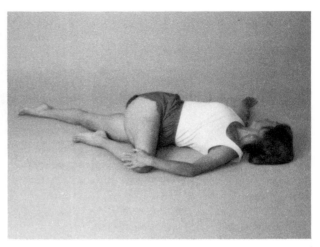

Spinal Twist on Back, One Leg Bent (First Position)          Spinal Twist on Back, One Leg Bent (Second Position)

your left shoulder and chest slightly off the carpet. While pressing the elbow and lifting, slightly twist the upper torso to the right; your right shoulder will come closer to the carpet and you will feel more of a stretch. Place a pillow under your head if your head is arched back or uncomfortable. I call this the "universal stretch" in class because it stretches so many areas and feels so good!

Now take three *Three-Part Rhythmic Breaths,* feeling the stretch in the ribcage area while holding the breath, and relaxing into the rotation of the lower back on the exhalation. Relax out of the position and repeat the stretch to the other side.

This is an excellent releaser for the spine, the chest, and especially the lower back. There should be no pain in the lower back. If there is, make sure you are not arching there. The purpose of shifting the hips towards the bent knee is to prevent the arch.

# DEEP RELAXATION

## Meditative Deep Relaxation

Results from this form of relaxation are more profound if you are proficient in the first two types of deep relaxation. Students have been "surprised" and "amazed" at the power of this technique. An associate at the University of California sat in on my classes and experienced a deeper level of mental and emotional release than she had ever experienced with other techniques. Several times a year I demonstrate the technique in her class in Sports Physiology. Her students have a similar, enthusiastic response. In this form of relaxation you are essentially practicing a form of concentration/meditation. The challenge of this technique is to silence the chatter of your mind. While the progressive muscle relaxation technique taught in *Week One* is best if you are trying to relax physically, *Passive Deep Relaxation* and *Meditative Deep Relaxation* cause deeper release on the emotional/mental levels.

*Meditative Deep Relaxation* is considered the most beneficial of all the exercises for relieving anxiety. It takes you a step deeper into mental relaxation than *Active* or *Passive Deep Relaxation*. If it is done correctly, you will experience a deep physical and mental peace. Your metabolism will slow down and your mind will quiet.

This form of deep relaxation is an outgrowth of both Herbert Benson's meditation technique of observing the breath and counting "one" or a word of the practitioner's choice on each exhalation [7,8] and my own experience and research on meditation.

**Caution**: Do not practice meditative relaxation or meditation if you are deeply depressed; rather, take a walk in a pleasant setting, practice the exercises, or seek support from a friend or counselor.

## The R-E-L-A-X-ation Meditation

Begin by coming into a comfortable seated position, or stretching out on your back, as in the previous deep relaxations. Inhale, and tense your whole body. Exhale, and relax your body. Repeat two more times, increasing the tension each time you inhale. Follow this with three slow, *Three-Part Rhythmic Breaths*.

Now focus your attention on your breathing. Do not control your breath. Let it follow its own natural rhythm. You may find that in becoming aware of your breathing rhythm you start to control it. Continue to practice until you no longer attempt to control the rhythm of your breath. The object is to observe and experience the breathing, not to change or control it. Be aware of the rise and fall of the abdominal area and chest as you breathe. For approximately a minute, be attentive to these bodily movements as you breathe. Notice that in this relaxed position your stomach will rise as you inhale and slightly contract as you exhale.

Next become aware of the breath at the tip of your nose, as it enters the nasal passages. Feel the thin stream of air coming in and going out. Notice the coolness of the air as you inhale and the warmth of the air as you exhale. Focus at the tip of your nose for approximately one minute.

Now draw your attention to the exhalation. For the next minute, consciously relax the body more deeply with each exhalation. On the exhalation, mentally say the word "relaxing" and experience the body relaxing from head to toe. Visualize wave after wave of the ocean washing through you, releasing the residual tension.

Now focus on erasing remaining thoughts with each exhalation. Visualize a blackboard with your thoughts written on it. With each exhalation mentally say the word "erasing" and watch the thoughts being removed. Use your breathing, the mental repetition, and the visualization to hold your concentration in the present. Practice for approximately one minute.

Next focus your attention at your heart and visualize a valentine heart bound by colorful string. As you cut the cords, mentally say the words "letting go" on the exhalation. Watch the heart grow and expand as it frees itself. Let go of constricting emotions. Let each cut of a string represent a letting go of a binding negative emotion.

When you feel ready to shift your attention (after a minute or so), mentally say the word "accepting" as you exhale. Visualize yourself. See yourself being accepted by others. The visualization might be of a specific person accepting you, or a group of friends, or even you accepting yourself. Have the visualization fit your current needs. Perhaps your situation warrants a visualization of you accepting someone else.

Lastly, as you begin to feel more at peace with yourself physically, mentally, and emotionally, let your peace expand, by repeating "expanding peace" with each breath. Say "expanding" as you inhale, and "peace" as you exhale. Visualize yourself as a wave of peace expanding and dissolving into a great ocean of peace. Let the barriers of separation and stress be released and come into your core of inner silence and tranquility.

Take ten minutes for the whole meditation exercise. End by enjoying several minutes without the focus on the breath. Experience the peaceful state of your mind and body. You have relaxed

**WATCH THE BREATH**
Do not control your breath. Let it follow its own natural rhythm. You may find that in becoming aware of your breathing rhythm you start to control it.

into the relaxation response and can witness what it feels like. Take a few minutes before returning to your activities.

You may want to put this and other relaxation/meditations on a tape. If you prefer not to, one way to remember this meditation is to note the letters that spell out **RELAX:**

"**R**elax" = *Relax from head to toe, in a wave of release.*
"**E**rase" = *Erase all thoughts on your mental blackboard.*
"**L**et Go" = *Let go emotionally. Cut the bindings of your heart.*
"**A**ccept" = *Accept yourself or others as you, or they, are.*
"e**X**pand into Peace" = *Expand into your Self.*

FOR STUDENTS IN MY STRESS MANAGEMENT CLASSES, I recommend using the calm, clear state arrived at through the practice of the deep relaxation/meditation techniques to:

1. Enjoy the peaceful state you have achieved for several minutes, or

2. Reevaluate any aspect of your life which is stressful, or

3. Pray/meditate according to your own spiritual training or inclination.

## REWARDING YOURSELF

ASSIGN AND GIVE YOURSELF appropriate, positive reinforcement. It might be assigning yourself fewer tasks for the day. It might be a creative project you thought you did not have time to do. If you are not enjoying the process of living, of day-to-day existence, choose an activity that will rekindle your enthusiasm. You have duties and responsibilities, but all work and no play cause stress symptomology. Hours in a waiting room of a doctor's office, physical examinations, and x-rays are time consuming and costly. They are possibilities unless you make changes in your circumstances or in your perceptions.

## WEEKLY REVIEW

### Lesson Summary
We cannot keep going at a faster and faster pace and remain healthy. Balance your life with mini-vacations of personal quiet time, meditation or deep relaxation. Stop *doing*, and *be*. Experience the present in an enjoyable form for a minimum of ten minutes daily. This may mean simply announcing to your family you are taking a ten-minute "time out." Close the door, and perhaps listen to soothing music, meditate, or practice deep relaxation. This is not a time to ruminate, make lists, or *do* anything.

# CHARTING YOUR PROGRESS

| MON | TUES | WED | THUR | FRI | SAT | SUN | RELAXATION SKILL |
|---|---|---|---|---|---|---|---|
| | | | | | | | BREATHING EXERCISES |
| | | | | | | | PHYSICAL EXERCISES |
| | | | | | | | DEEP RELAXATION |
| | | | | | | | INSTANT STRESS RELEASER |
| | | | | | | | OTHER STRESS-REDUCING ACTIVITY (Jogging, listening to calming music, etc.) |
| | | | | | | | LEVEL OF STRESS (Rate on a scale of 1-10) |

**Directions:** Place an X after each relaxation skill you practiced for that day. Evaluate your stress level at the end of each day on a scale of 1-10, with 10 representing a high level of stress. Review at the end of the week and note which techniques have been the most beneficial for you.

1) Sitting Spinal Stretches (In Three Positions)

2) The Rope Climb

3) Shoulder and Chest Stretch (First and Second Positions)

3) Shoulder and Chest Stretch (Advanced Position)

4) Straight Arm Rotations

5) Standing Forward Bend (In Two Positions)

6) Spinal Twist on Back, One Leg Bent (In Two Positions)

7) The R-E-L-A-X-ation Meditation (With Alternate Position)

**WEEK FOUR**

# LESSON FOUR: PERCEPTION AND SELF-ESTEEM IN STRESS MANAGEMENT

## The Key to Stress Management: How We Perceive a Given Situation

Our emotional responses and physical behavior are based on our perception of a situation. This perception is colored by our attitudes, values, beliefs, and upbringing. We then select an emotion appropriate to the way in which we have labeled (perceived) a situation.

According to Albert Ellis, a cognitive therapist who developed Rational Emotive Therapy, it is not the situation that causes the psychological distress, but the perception of that situation. In an A-B-C format, A is the situation or "activating event," B is the perception or "belief" about the situation, and C is the emotional response or "consequence." Ellis states that C is the result of B, not of A. It is the belief or perception of an event, rather than the event itself, which causes psychological distress (see the illustration "The Power of Thought" on the following page).

A situation cannot always be changed, but you can gain control over how you respond to any set of circumstances. To reduce stress, challenge the irrational and perfectionist statements you may be making to yourself. This week's instant stress releaser is to observe your thoughts and become aware of their patterns. Utilize this information to change the internal language you use to describe a given circumstance. The result is reduced stress-related emotional and physical responses.

Do you find yourself mentally saying "I should," or "I ought to," or "I must"? Are you labeling as "catastrophic" the inability to meet unrealistic goals? Although life is neither easy nor fair, it is not catastrophic nor disastrous. Challenge a thought pattern if your evaluation or belief about a given situation needs to be tempered. Internal, unrealistic standards and demands can result in stressful emotions which lead to stress-related illnesses.

# A SITUATION
The activating event.

# B PERCEPTION
Our perception or belief about the situation.

*Our internal language describes the situation. Our perceptions are based on: Attitudes • Beliefs • Habits • Values • Conditioning*

**THE POWER OF THOUGHT**

# C CONSEQUENCE
Our emotional response and resulting behavior.

DISCOVER THE A-B-C STEPS IN YOUR OWN LIFE. Once you are aware of how you experience stress and the situation that arouses that stress, write down the thoughts involved. Catch the fleeting thought you have in the space between the situation and the emotional response. This thought is often part of our general approach to life, and is summed up in a flash of perception. It is a pattern which over the years has become a reflex response to a given situation. Become the objective observer of yourself, especially of your thinking habits.

Once you become aware of a thought, you can analyze it. Is it an irrational or perfectionist demand that causes the tension? Writing out your thoughts will clarify what they are and how often you make the same statements to yourself. The quiet time technique of *Meditative Deep Relaxation* helps you to distance yourself from your views, to be more of an unbiased observer of yourself. From this perspective, see if you are imposing on yourself statements of limitation and anxiety.

Transactional Analysis is another psychotherapeutic method which investigates cognitive structure and the emotions. The format starts with recognition of thought patterns. Once the internal language which arouses stress is observed, the ego states are labeled Parent, Adult, or Child. Is it early parental injunctions that you have

internalized? Are the *oughts, shoulds,* and *musts* theirs? Do you want to continue living your parents' views and standards? Although freedom of choice does carry with it a degree of anxiety, there is greater stress in fulfilling their expectations than in discovering and living by your own value system.

Perhaps your perceptions are based on early decisions you made as a child in response to your parents' injunctions. Is your striving for perfection actually a continuation of trying to please your parents and win their affection? These decisions were once useful, but are they functional for you now? The answers lie in self-observation and in the resulting increased self-knowledge.

Once you are aware of your thought patterns, the choice of making changes is in your hands. Think **YES** to yourself: **Y**ou **E**ase **S**tress. Perception, attitude, how you approach life is your choice. You know your thoughts better than anyone else. Using the tools of conscious breathing, stretching, and deep relaxation to be more in the present moment, you will become better able to catch those fleeting, destructive thought patterns. After becoming aware of thoughts preceding an emotion, investigate the background of those thoughts, the childhood experiences that created your mental tape or emotional response.

If these techniques do not work for you, and you have one thought that keeps repeating itself over and over, try the "thought stopping" technique. It consists of inwardly shouting "stop!" to thoughts that crop up habitually. There is no analysis of the thought pattern; simply stop the thought. This technique is not a repression of feelings but a stopping of a recognized or repeated thought pattern that is causing unwanted stress. You can choose to stand at the gateway of your mind and decide which thoughts to entertain and which thoughts to hold at bay.

Another effective technique I use regularly is affirmations. If I find myself making a negative internal statement, I immediately change the thought to its positive opposite. "I am ugly, dumb, old, or tired" becomes a positive affirmation of beauty, intelligence, youthful outlook, or enthusiasm for life. A boring, hectic, or depressing situation can be turned into a fascinating or challenging circumstance by an initial change of thought. This is not to deny the reality of a difficult situation, but to perceive a glimmer of the positive and build on it. I counsel my clients to turn their attention in a new, positive direction and give energy to that. For example, when a client is unsuccessful in losing weight, I suggest focusing on how to eat for good health and maximum energy, rather than focusing on the bulge and calorie count. Ultimately, stress management is conscious choice in thought. *The fabric of our lives is woven from the minute threads of perception we choose to hold.*

**YOU ARE IN CONTROL**
Once you are aware of your thought patterns, the choice of making changes is in your hands.

## Self-Esteem and Stress Management

In my work as a counselor I have observed the importance of self-esteem in stress management. Our perception of ourselves and our view of our relationship to the rest of the world deeply colors our perceptions of present-day situations. A person with low self-esteem is habitually overwhelmed by a given stressor. A change in the environment is interpreted as an obstacle in life. A person who has self-confidence and enthusiasm often interprets the same stressor as a challenge or opportunity for personal growth. The chart below graphically describes the impact of self-esteem on thought.

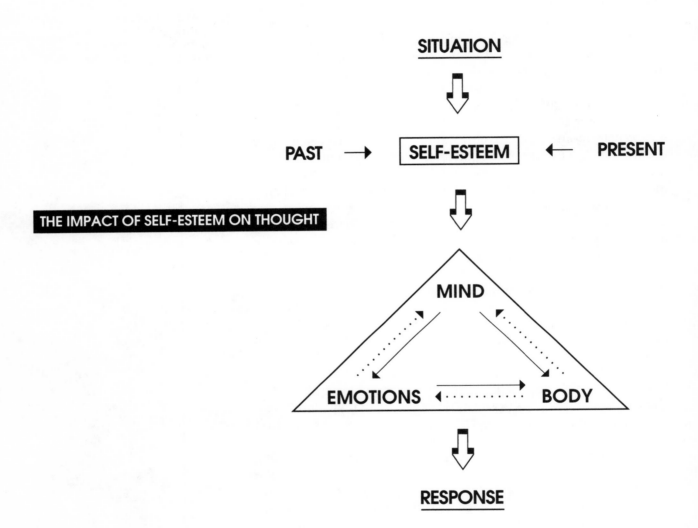

IN THE LATE 1980'S DR. SUZANNE KOBASA discovered the "Hardiness Personality," a person who has three qualities which enable him/her to cope effectively with stress. The Hardiness Personality was developed from Dr. Kobasa's research on lawyers and executives handling rigorous demands successfully (i.e., without their getting run-down and developing serious illness). The Hardiness Personality expresses the three attitudes of control, challenge, and commitment. These qualities, which largely reflect high self-esteem, can be developed. Use the therapeutic methods

above for changing perceptions and then self-actualize a Hardiness Personality. You are giving energy to characteristics within yourself which are there, but have withered from lack of attention and nurturing. As human potential writer and lecturer Donald Walters states, live as if you possess a quality and it becomes your own. For example, rather than setting a goal of becoming calm, act with calmness now, no matter how imperfectly you perform it initially. After reading the description of each trait, follow the suggestions for developing this trait within yourself.

## TRAITS TO DEVELOP FOR COPING WITH STRESS

### Commitment

Individuals who have commitment in life are those who find an aspect of their lives deeply meaningful. Involvement gives them the strength to endure life's pressures with greater calmness. Having commitment gives purpose and direction to their lives. Rather than an underlying current of alienation or separation, there is a sense of being connected to the world around them through that commitment. They are drawn out of themselves into being part of a larger whole.

The underlying enthusiasm behind commitment strengthens the immune system. When one has no more reason to get up in the morning than to earn enough to pay the bills, he easily slips into either short-term or long-term stress. As mentioned earlier, stress weakens the immune system, the body's complex defense system which protects you from invading bacteria, viruses, or their toxic products. According to Dr. Laurence Badgley, author of *Healing AIDS Naturally*, the natural killer cells of the immune system are weakened by bereavement, depression, loneliness, separation from a parent, and acute and chronic stress.

If your life is flat and you lack enthusiasm, begin to explore new avenues of expression or interest. Investigate a forgotten interest you "haven't had time for." Write a wish list of things you would like to do if money or time were not an issue. Within that list lies the potential for greater happiness, health, and joy. Focusing on the larger dream and taking the first tangible steps can change the way you deal with daily pressures.

One of my clients was responding to the trials in her life with general malaise. She found it difficult to get out of bed in the morning. After each long night of fitful sleep and anxious dreams she awoke tired and overwhelmed. She barely had the strength to drag herself through each day. Through counseling and self-appraisal she realized that in the overload of being a working, single parent, she had given up hopes of ever pursuing her dreamed-of career.

**RENEW YOUR ENTHUSIASM FOR LIFE**
If your life is flat and you lack enthusiasm, begin to explore new avenues of expression or interest. Investigate a forgotten interest you "haven't had time for."

Although it took five years of evening courses and economic hardship, she acquired the degree and experience to make her vision a reality. What I observed was that, in the process, her attitude towards the stressors in her life shifted. While she pursued the long-range goal, the daily traumas became more peripheral, and she became enthusiastic and energetic in her response to life.

The following poem by Goethe inspires and beautifully expresses the impact commitment can have on your life.

## *Commitment*

*Until one is committed, there is hesitancy,*
*the chance to draw back, always ineffectiveness.*
*Concerning all acts of initiative there is one elementary truth*
*the ignorance of which kills countless ideas and endless plans:*
*that the moment one definitively commits oneself*
*then Providence moves too.*
*All sorts of things occur to help one*
*that would never otherwise have occurred.*
*A whole stream of events issues from the decision,*
*raising in one's favor all manner of unforeseen incidents*
*and meetings and material assistance,*
*which no man could have dreamed would come his way.*
*Whatever you can do or dream you can, begin it!*
*Boldness has genius, power, and magic in it.*

*—GOETHE*

### Challenge

The second trait expressed by the Hardiness Personality is the ability to see obstacles in life as challenges. This personality has the self-confidence to look for creative answers to difficult problems. According to the June 1989 *Brain/Mind Bulletin,* when a person perceives a problematic event as a challenge and is confident that there is a solution, epinephrine and noradrenalin levels increase. This response reduces levels of adrenalin and cortisol, the hormones associated with anxiety and stress.

This trait can be developed by observing areas where you have always assumed your inability to accomplish a task. Then, accepting the risk of failure in relatively insignificant areas, attempt the challenge. This develops self-confidence and a positive approach as a natural response to new and more challenging circumstances. It is learning how to say "Yes" to life rather than an automatic "No" to life. In one stress management class I suggested to the students that they attempt something they had never done before. The following week a woman said she had installed a new windshield wiper for the first time. This little act made her feel good about herself, and this feeling spilled into other areas of her life. Each week look for

little ways to challenge the potential within yourself. (Potential talent can develop only if you use it.)

In my own life, I internalized my father's lack of confidence in being able to understand things mechanical. Each time I dare to learn a new skill in this area I feel a surge of well-being and independence. This happened when I taught myself how to use the mysterious computer and the complex sewing machine, and to change a tire myself. These little "successes" have enabled me not to shut down when a piece of equipment breaks down. These past experiences have also enabled me to be open to challenges in other areas of my life.

## Control

The third trait of a Hardiness Personality is control, the attitude that one's input into a situation can influence events. Rather than feeling overwhelmed by circumstances, Hardiness Personalities believe they can affect any given situation. This attitude takes them out of a passive role into an active one. They are no longer victims of life but contributors to it.

One of my clients was despondent after she was diagnosed as having a life-threatening disease. She anxiously followed the complex instructions of her physician and complied with all his suggestions on how she ought to live her life. Rather than taking part in the healing process, she put her health solely in her doctor's hands. Her anxiety and tension became part of the illness. After counseling and encouragement, she began to see the need to take an active role. It was wonderful to see her transformation as she explored new avenues of health and healing. When she was later diagnosed as terminally ill, she continued to remain both positive and active, even in the process of dying. At the time of her passing, she left with a sense of dignity and control.

## Being Centered

In my seminars I suggest that the quality of being "on center" is as essential to stress management as those of challenge, commitment, and control. Being "on center" means recognizing, honoring, and expressing our essential potential or Spirit within. This core of our being often is devalued in youth and neglected in adulthood. Stress-filled living results in our "not being ourselves," expressing from our anxious, overworked, or fatigued periphery.

The work of stress management is to allow our inner calm and caring strength to be expressed in our relationships, work, and creativity. The stress management tools of conscious breathing, stretching, deep relaxation, meditation, and perceptual reframing enable us to broaden the limited perspective we have of ourselves and life around us. We have the choice of living from our center or our periphery every moment of our lives. The challenge is to remember to express from our deepest potential rather than from

**NOT BEING OURSELVES**
Stress-filled living results in our "not being ourselves," expressing from our anxious, overworked, or fatigued periphery.

our surface. To do so allows the calmness and harmony within to come to the forefront when they are most needed: when we are inundated by stress.

## Perceptual Exercises

The instant stress releaser assignments accelerate progress made through the practice of the exercise and relaxation techniques. Practice the perceptual exercises along with the weekly routines. They take no extra time because they are lessons in self-observation. They train you first to see your physical and mental stress patterns and then give you tools to change them.

The routines, or your creative expression of them, may be all you need. I have heard repeated "success" stories, from students and clients alike, that these stress-reducing techniques "changed their lives." I have seen faces so changed by the practice of these techniques that no words needed to be spoken. With years of tension dropped away, people feel "alive again." For the five weeks of this program, though, do experiment with the instant stress releaser assignments. The insights gained from the assignments will facilitate your long-term stress management.

## The purpose of the assignments is to help you become aware of:

A. How you physically experience stress;

B. What situations trigger your stress symptoms;

C. The thoughts that cause your stressful emotional/physical response; and

D. What you can do to change your mental, emotional, and physical patterns of stress.

In my experience as a counselor, I have discovered there is no system or approach that can reach everyone. There are no pat answers or easy solutions. For one person, stress is released by getting in touch with unexpressed emotions. For another, stress is reduced by a change in behavior. In another, it takes a cognitive change to relax the tension. Each of the instant stress releasers emphasizes one of these aspects.

## The Challenge of Change

The breathing, exercises, relaxation, and quiet time practices give you specific ways to release physical, emotional, and mental tension. But perceptions often become habitual ways of viewing oneself and life's situations. These perceptions are comfortable. To break out of a mold that is secure and safe, even when debilitating, takes courage and commitment. It takes effort to lift oneself out of a rut and go against the current of habit. As Mark Twain said, "Giving up smoking is easy. I've done it a thousand times."

It is challenging to trade a predictable pattern of thought or

behavior for a new, but uncertain one. The techniques work. They help cut through the layers of anxiety and stress, but how do you gain the fortitude to persevere? Our minds resist duties, assignments, and imposed structuring. Give the five-week program over to your mind's natural habit of investigation and exploration. These stress management techniques for well-being will become a natural part of your lifestyle if you let your mind take part in the process of adaptation and creativity.

Are you afraid of the quiet time techniques? Perhaps you are worrying about unleashing impulses you now control, or perhaps you fear what might be found inside yourself. The techniques are both valuable and safe. The conscious mind, even when relaxed, will not allow more than you can handle to bubble to the surface. You may feel a wave of anger or sadness as you relax the barrier to your subconscious mind, but a release of these emotions will be healing for you. Only those who are clinically depressed, psychotic, or hallucinating need to avoid *Meditative Deep Relaxation* and *Quiet Time* practices. Additional support, beyond the confines of this book, may be needed. Professional help is available through therapists, counselors, corporate programs, and ministers or priests.

## Personality Restructuring

Psychologists disagree whether or not we can restructure our personalities. A person with an "A type" personality is defined by Friedman and Rosenman as one who is prone to anger and hostility, compulsively competitive, and impatient. Their classic definition of a person with a "B type" personality is one who is easygoing, unhurried, and content. Can we change from an "A type" to a "B type"? Friedman, who teaches stress management programs and defines himself as a self-reconstructed "A type," believes you can. [25]

Methods taught in this program can expand your awareness to include previously unconscious needs, emotions, and conflicts. An increased understanding of yourself opens the door to changes in behavior, thought, and emotion. The process contributes to an integration of feelings, thoughts, and behavior, whether or not it is labeled personality restructuring. This harmonizing of the different aspects of yourself enhances inner peace and your relationship to the world around you. Anxiety, depression, and other stress symptomologies are signals warning of imbalances that need correction. You have inner resources which can be tapped to help you cope with stress. By using the tools offered in this program, you can reclaim your calmness and strength.

An "A type" personality is often successful in what he does. The goal is to keep the enthusiasm and productivity of an "A type" without the physiological costs or hostility that come from an unrelenting fast pace. No one wants to develop such varied stress symptoms as ulcers, headaches, cardiovascular illnesses, or insomnia. What is "success" if the cost is your health and well-being?

# INSTANT STRESS RELEASER

## Gaining Awareness of Internal Language

Each week's instant stress releaser builds on the previous one. This week's assignment is to catch the thought that triggers the stressful emotional/physical response to a situation. Continue your practice of observing what situations trigger a stressful response, what your stressful response is, and developing concentration in a present activity. This week also observe the thought process at the time of increased stress. Keep a list of the perceptions you have just before your emotional or physical response to a situation.

As you continue to practice concentrating on a present activity, it will become easier to catch the fleeting thought before an emotional response. It is an interesting paradox that the more you get involved in the present moment, the more you become an observer of that moment. This will help you catch long-held perceptions that you are hardly aware of thinking.

# BREATHING EXERCISE

## Double Breath

The *Double Breath* and the *Bellows Breath* (taught in *Week Five*) are introduced for their stimulating and invigorating effect. Stress is, at times, expressed by boredom, chronic fatigue, burnout, or depression. These breathing techniques, coupled with the exercises, help to increase vitality and enthusiasm.

The *Double Breath* is excellent for removing residual tension in the body. It allows intake of a maximum amount of oxygen in the shortest amount of time and enhances oxygen/carbon dioxide exchange. A similar breath is used by long distance runners. It tones all the muscles utilized in breathing and is superb training for gaining control of the respiratory muscles. When you are feeling a lack of vitality, if you are bored, depressed or fatigued, take three *Double Breaths* and observe the effects.

The inhalation is through the nostrils and the exhalation is through the mouth. All three sections of the lungs are used. Inhale through the nostrils with a double inhalation. The first phase is short and involves the abdomen and lower ribs. Take a second inhalation (with no exhalation in between) and expand fully through the rib cage area and upper lungs. In the first phase of the inhalation count one; in the second phase count to four.

The exhalation is the same, but in reverse and through the mouth. In the first phase of the exhalation relax the throat and begin contraction of the ribs; in the second phase of the exhalation continue contraction of the ribs and add contraction of the abdominal muscles. Completely squeeze out the carbon dioxide from the lower portion of the lungs.

Repeat the *Double Breath* three times. Once you feel comfortable with it and sense the rhythm, no longer count. Let the short/long rhythm be natural. Practice with a straight spine, relaxed shoulders, and open chest.

## *WEEK FOUR ROUTINE*

Three-Part Rhythmic Breath
Double Breath
Alternate Shoulder Lifts
Shoulder Stretch
The Rabbit
The Camel
Side Stretch
The Butterfly
Sitting Forward Bend
Seated Spinal Twist
Lower Back Release
The Circulatory Shake
The Circulatory Stimulator
Meditative Deep Relaxation on Sound

AFTER READING AND PRACTICING THE NEXT SECTION, *Detailed Instructions on the Exercises,* use the At-A-Glance illustrations at the end of this chapter as a quick reference to remember the exercises. Although this course emphasizes integrating the stretches, breathing, and deep relaxation into your day, when and if you do have the time, take fifteen to twenty minutes out of your day to enjoy the benefits of a full routine and deep relaxation. You will be surprised by the sense of well-being you will experience.

# DETAILED INSTRUCTIONS
# ON WEEK FOUR EXERCISES

### Three-Part Rhythmic Breath

Practice the *Three-Part Rhythmic Breath* for its calming effect. Within ten breaths the body and mind can be quieted. This technique is excellent before going into an interview, performing, or engaging in any other stressful event.

A relaxed body and clear mind coupled with anticipation maximize performance level. One of my students, the number one golfer on the University of California golf team, uses this breath to calm himself before each crucial play. Under pressure in international competition, he has repeatedly quieted his anxiety to allow peak performance. He keeps coming back to my classes because the breathing and stretching have tangible results.

Begin this week's routine sitting on the carpet on the edge of a pillow with your eyes closed. Take a minute to focus on the present, letting go of worries of the future or the past. This is your time to stretch out your tensions and relax. With your eyes closed, take three three-part rhythmic breaths. Inhale deeply, hold the breath an equal count, and then exhale to an equal count. Fully contract the abdominal muscles in completing the exhalation. Pause before beginning the next inhalation.

Alternate Shoulder Lifts

### Double Breaths

Practice three *Double Breaths* (page 90), inhaling short/long through the nose, and exhaling short/long through the mouth.

### Alternate Shoulder Lifts

Remain in a seated position. With your eyes closed, focus your attention and feel what is happening in the area being stretched. As you inhale, lift one shoulder up as high as you can toward your ear. Hold and tense the shoulder in this position as you hold your breath. As you exhale, let the shoulder drop down to its original position. Now do the other side. Repeat each side two more times.

### Shoulder Stretch

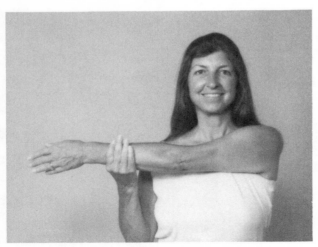
Shoulder Stretch

Bring your left arm across your chest and grasp your forearm with your right hand. Gently lengthen the left arm as you pull it towards your chest. Hold it there as you take three *Diaphragmatic Breaths*. Keep your chest lifted as you breath. Repeat to the other side.

## The Rabbit

**First Position:** Come into a kneeling position, sitting on your heels. Have your right big toe over your left big toe and the heels apart, so that your feet cradle your buttocks. Sit firmly, yet lift through the torso, and let your legs relax. Place your right palm over your left with the thumbs touching. If you feel pressure on your ankles or your knees, place a pillow or rolled blanket between your legs and sit on it. Take three *Complete Breaths* in this position. The venous blood is squeezed out of tired legs. When the position is released, fresh oxygenated blood flows into them.

**Second Position:** Drop your hands to your side. On your next exhalation bend forward from the hips with a flat back and rest your forehead on the floor. There are two alternatives to completing the second position. Experiment with the first and second alternatives, and choose which one works best for you. Both emphasize releasing tension in the shoulders and neck.

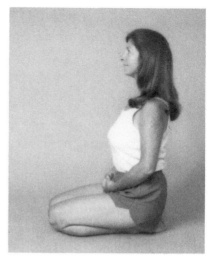

The Rabbit (First Position)

The Rabbit (First Alternate Position)

The Rabbit (Second Alternate Position)

**First Alternate:** Clasp your hands on your buttocks and rock up onto the top of your head by lifting your buttocks off your feet. Bring your arms over your head toward the floor. Hold for three breaths and then relax back down to your heels. Keeping a flat back, slowly return to the first position, the seated position with a flat back.

**Second Alternate:** While resting your chest on your thighs and forehead on the floor, grasp your feet with your thumbs around the tops of your feet and your fingers around the soles of your feet. Without letting go of your feet, lift your buttocks off your heels and roll onto the top of your head. The goal is to feel a stretch/tension in your shoulders and neck. To increase the stretch/tension bring your heels together, tuck your head closer to your knees, lengthen your neck by pulling your shoulders toward the ceiling, and keep pushing forward with your thighs.

For even more of a stretch, while lifting the shoulders towards the ceiling, pull the elbows toward the floor. If you still do not feel the stretch, bend your knees more, lowering your thighs several inches. Now bend your elbows and lock them. Without unlocking your bent elbows, raise the buttocks again. Take three breaths in this position and then lower down onto your heels and relax your arms, neck, and shoulders. Come back into the seated position with your back flat.

The Camel (First Position)

The Camel (Second Position)

The Camel (Third Position)

## The Camel

There are three variations to *The Camel*. Start with the first position and work up to the third position as your range of flexibility increases. Each variation stimulates circulation in the spine, expands the chest, releases shoulder and neck tension, and stretches the front of the thighs.

**First Position:** Sit on your heels and place your hands behind you at shoulder width with your fingers pointing away from your body. Tuck your chin to your chest and lift your buttocks off your heels. Tilt your pelvis by flattening your lower back and tightening your buttocks and abdominal muscles. Keeping your body in a straight line, take three complete breaths.

**Second Position:** From the first position, push the thighs higher, squeezing the buttocks and lifting the chest. To open more through the shoulders, keep lifting your chest toward the ceiling and press evenly into both hands. Let your facial muscles and neck relax. If you have no neck problems, and enough lift and arch in the chest, your head can relax back comfortably. Take three *Complete Breaths* in this position. To come out of the position, lower your body back down onto your buttocks.

**Third Position:** Start by kneeling with your body upright. Be perpendicular to the floor from your knees to the top of your head (Christian prayer position). Have your feet straight behind your knees so that there is no twist to your knees. Keeping the chin tucked to the chest, lift and arch the chest, and place one hand on one heel. Roll the chest towards the ceiling and place the other hand on the other heel. To protect the lower back and maintain the stretch in the upper back, keep the thighs parallel to each other and perpendicular to the carpet, and tighten the buttocks. Let the head relax back if it is comfortable for you. It should hang freely and not be overarched backward. The overarched neck occurs if you lack the flexibility in the chest and cannot lift and arch sufficiently to let the neck hang freely. Until you have the flexibility in the chest, keep the chin tucked towards the chest. Take three *Complete Breaths* in this position, working toward six *Complete Breaths*. With each inhalation, lift the chest toward the ceiling, and check to be sure the buttocks muscles are still tight and the thighs pushed forward, perpendicular to the carpet; with each exhalation, focus on relaxing the face and neck. To come out of the position, roll to the side and sit back down on your heels.

Alternatives to Vary the Intensity of the Back Arch:

1. To lessen the intensity of the stretch, curl your toes under (rather than having the tops of your feet against the carpet), before arching back.

2. Vary the width of the knees. The closer together the knees are, the greater the stretch in the spine. Start hip distance apart. Always have the ankles directly behind the knees.

## Side Stretch

Begin in the first position of *The Rabbit Pose* with your buttocks cradled between your feet and your spine upright. Place your arms at your sides. As you inhale, bring your arms straight out to the side (palms up) and over your head; as you exhale, interlock your fingers and roll the palms toward the ceiling. On the next inhalation, reach higher towards the ceiling. Pull down through the upper back muscles to open the shoulders and chest. As you exhale, drop your hips to the carpet on your right and lean your trunk toward the left. Take three to six *Diaphragmatic Breaths* in this position. With each inhalation stretch through the arms and lift through the chest; with each exhalation pull down through the upper back and relax more deeply into the side stretch. To come back to the original position, tighten your abdominals and lift your buttocks back onto your cradled heels. Repeat to the other side.

Side Stretch

## The Butterfly

Come into a seated position with your legs stretched out in front of you. Do three ankle rotations in each direction and then point and flex your feet several times.

Bend both knees to the chest with the soles of your feet on the carpet. Let the knees and hips relax outward so that the soles of the feet touch. Place your hands behind you and lift the lower back into correct posture. If you find that your lower back still sags back towards the carpet, sit on the edge of a pillow to keep the natural arch of the lumbar spine.

To increase the stretch in the groin and inner thighs, bring your

The Butterfly

hands to your ankles and lean forward from your hips. Pull up against your ankles, bending your elbows. Take six *Diaphragmatic Breaths* in this stretched position. Keep your mind focused on a correct extended spinal position on the inhalation and on relaxing the inner thigh muscles on the exhalation. Notice your shoulders. Do not hunch them. Slowly come out of the position and stretch your legs out in front of you.

If *The Butterfly* is difficult for you, and you find your lower back slumping, continue practice of the *Inner Thigh Stretch* on your back (page 50).

Sitting Forward Bend (First Position)

Sitting Forward Bend (Second Position)

## Sitting Forward Bend

**First Position:** This exercise stretches out tension in the lower back, behind the knees, and in the hamstrings. Begin by sitting (on the edge of a pillow if needed) with your legs stretched out in front of you. Keep your lower abdominal muscles tight throughout the exercise. Inhale, bringing your arms out to the side and then over your head with the palms facing each other; exhale, pulling your upper back muscles down. Inhale and lean back several inches with an erect spine and stretch through the arms and chest.

**Second Position:** Keeping the abdominal muscles tight, exhale and bend forward from the hips as far as you can without disturbing correct spinal alignment. Place your hands on your legs wherever they come naturally without scrunching up your shoulders or curling your spine. Do not sacrifice spinal alignment to get your head closer to your knees. Take six *Diaphragmatic Breaths* in this position.

Note the following details while in the stretch:

1. Keep your heels flexed, but do not push the backs of your knees to the carpet.

2. Notice if your chin is tucked or arched, and correct it so that it is a natural extension of your spine.

3. Push your heels in their flexed position toward the wall and your buttocks in the opposite direction.

4. In working towards the full stretch, first bring your pelvis

to your thighs, then your chest to your thighs, and lastly your head to your shins. It is a strain on your neck and spine if you curl your back to get your head to your knees.

To come out of the position, inhale and come up with a flat back and arms over your head. If your lower back is weak, come up with a curled spine, arms on your legs. Exhale, lowering your arms to your side.

## Seated Spinal Twist

This stretch is excellent for keeping the rotating muscles along the spine elastic. It releases lower back tension and increases lung capacity by stretching the intercostal muscles between the ribs.

Begin in a comfortable, cross-legged position, seated on the edge of a pillow. Place your left hand on the outside of your right thigh just above your knee, and the right hand on the carpet behind you, close to your hips. Take six *Complete Breaths* in this position. To take pressure off the spine, as you inhale press the right hand against the carpet and lift up out of your hips, observing correct spinal alignment. Keep the shoulders relaxed down and the chest open. As you exhale, press against your right leg with your left hand and relax into the rotation of the spine. Come back to the original seated position. Do not force the twist. Repeat to the other side.

To increase the rotation and expand the chest, use *Three-Part Rhythmic* breathing in the twisted position. As you hold the breath, the intercostal muscles are stretched. As you exhale, you will feel an increase in the rotation of the spine. Keep your attention on the spine to prevent over rotation.

Seated Spinal Twist

## Lower Back Release

This exercise is excellent for relief of several types of lower back aches. It stretches the muscles along the thigh and buttock which attach to the lumbar spine.

Lie on your back with a pillow under your head, your knees bent, and your feet by your buttocks. Bend your left knee into the chest; then turn the knee out to the side and place the ankle on the right thigh near the knee. Lift your right foot off the carpet and reach under your left knee with your left hand and around your right thigh with your right hand. Clasp your hands around your right shin.

If you cannot comfortably reach your right leg, continue practice of the exercise using a chair or wall as taught in *Week Two*. If you want more of a stretch, tighten your abdominal muscles and lift your head towards your knees.

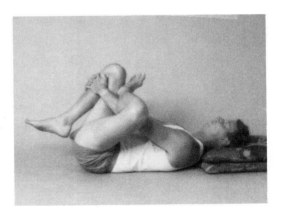

Lower Back Release

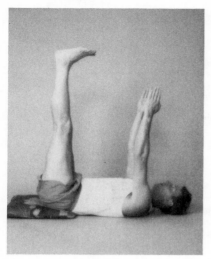

The Circulatory Shake

## The Circulatory Shake

This technique and the following one are based on two circulatory techniques taught to me by Ijima Senseii, Japan's foremost yoga teacher. He recommends practicing them every day for improving circulation and relaxation.

Begin by stretching out on your back. Raise your arms and legs perpendicular to the floor. Have your palms facing each other. Tense your legs (with the heels flexed) and arms. Shake them rapidly and vigorously in little one-inch movements for a full minute. The wrists and ankles remain stiff; the shaking is accomplished with a slight (one-inch) bending and straightening in the knees and elbows. Bring the arms and legs down to the floor and experience the sensations of released tensions and increased circulation.

If you cannot hold your legs perpendicular to the floor comfortably, place a pillow under your buttocks and bend your knees slightly.

The Circulatory Stimulator (First Part)

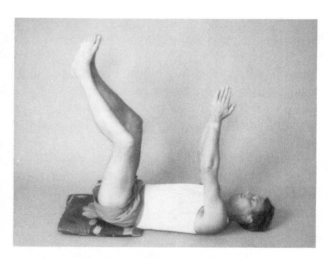

The Circulatory Stimulator (Second Part)

## The Circulatory Stimulator

**First Part:** Remaining on your back, bend your knees to your chest and bring the soles of your feet together. At the same time, bring your hands to your chest in a prayer position.

**Second Part:** Extend your arms and legs toward the ceiling, keeping the palms of the hands and the soles of the feet together. Bring them back to the original position close to your trunk. Repeat the first part and second part as rapidly as you can (approximately forty times) for a full minute. Relax your legs and arms back to the floor and experience the stimulating yet relaxing effect. Place a pillow under your buttocks during the exercise to protect your lower back.

# DEEP RELAXATION

## Meditative Deep Relaxation on Sound

Take a comfortable seated position in a chair or on the carpet or lie down in the deep relaxation position. Begin with three *Double Breaths*. With the first breath tense gently as you double inhale and relax as you double exhale. Increase the tension on the double inhalation in the next two breaths. Follow this with three *Three-Part Rhythmic* breaths, relaxing more deeply with each exhalation.

With your body relaxed, focus your attention on the sounds around you: the distant traffic or a nearby bird, or the quiet hum of voices in the next room. Then, gradually, a sound at a time, observe the most subtle sound you can hear. Remain attentive to that sound until you become aware of a subtler sound; then focus your attention there. As you listen, you will begin to hear your breath and the internal sounds of your body, such as your heartbeat and blood circulating. Eventually you will hear/feel more subtle sounds. Each time your mind wanders bring it back to listening. Make it a passive listening without intellectualizing on what you hear, or placing value judgments on what you are doing. The quality associated with this inner listening is one of being receptive, open to what is experienced. In this process, the personal traumas of the day are left behind and your body and state of mind become relaxed and peaceful. End the process by first letting go of the technique and experiencing the tranquil, clear state you have reached. Take a *Complete Breath,* open your eyes, and gently tense and relax your body. Step into your day with this perspective.

# REWARDING YOURSELF

HAVE YOU GIVEN YOURSELF a stress releasing reward each week for your efforts in managing your stress? Look at your processing of this aspect of the course. Are you giving yourself time in your life to enjoy it with stress relieving activities? Are you skipping this part of the program because it is a "waste of time"? Observe your response and possibly learn a lesson about yourself.

# WEEKLY REVIEW

## Lesson Summary
The key to stress management is attitude. Our evaluation of a given situation affects our emotions and behavior. Observe your thought patterns for needed changes in negative internal language. If it feels appropriate, analyze the roots of these patterns and then practice thought-stopping or affirmations to replace the irrational thought or negative attitude.

Self-esteem often colors our view of a stressor. Practicing the Hardiness Personality traits of commitment, challenge, and control enables you to better cope with daily stress.

# CHARTING YOUR PROGRESS

| MON | TUES | WED | THUR | FRI | SAT | SUN | **RELAXATION SKILL** |
|-----|------|-----|------|-----|-----|-----|----------------------|
| ☐ | ☐ | ☐ | ☐ | ☐ | ☐ | ☐ | BREATHING EXERCISES |
| ☐ | ☐ | ☐ | ☐ | ☐ | ☐ | ☐ | PHYSICAL EXERCISES |
| ☐ | ☐ | ☐ | ☐ | ☐ | ☐ | ☐ | DEEP RELAXATION |
| ☐ | ☐ | ☐ | ☐ | ☐ | ☐ | ☐ | INSTANT STRESS RELEASER |
| ☐ | ☐ | ☐ | ☐ | ☐ | ☐ | ☐ | OTHER STRESS-REDUCING ACTIVITY (Jogging, listening to calming music, etc.) |
| ☐ | ☐ | ☐ | ☐ | ☐ | ☐ | ☐ | LEVEL OF STRESS (Rate on a scale of 1-10) |

**Directions:** Place an X after each relaxation skill you practiced for that day. Evaluate your stress level at the end of each day on a scale of 1-10, with 10 representing a high level of stress. Review at the end of the week and note which techniques have been the most beneficial for you.

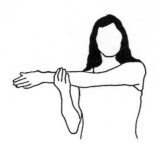

1) Alternate Shoulder Lifts          2) Shoulder Stretch

3) The Rabbit (With First and Second Alternate Positions)

4) The Camel (In Three Positions)

7) Sitting Forward Bend

5) Side Stretch

6) The Butterfly

8) Seated Spinal Twist

9) Lower Back Release

10) The Circulatory Shake

11) The Circulatory Stimulator (In Two Positions)

12) Meditative Deep Relaxation on Sound
(With Alternate Position)

WEEK FIVE

# LESSON FIVE: NUTRITIONAL TOOLS FOR STRESS MANAGEMENT

## Social Traditions

Food is deeply rooted in family traditions and reflects personal habits and needs. Integrating dietary changes into your life may not be appropriate at this time. Choose only those suggestions that feel compatible with your approach to nutrition and will aid in reducing your stress. If a suggestion leads to increased stress, let go of the strategy. One battle plan does not work in all cases. The following recommendations in nutrition have scientific support, but if they do not apply to you, or if they frustrate you, remember, you are the most knowledgeable about what works for you.

Nutrition is a vast subject and volumes have been written on the subject. This lesson focuses on eating habits that reduce stress, and presents an optimal nutritional approach for stress management. Making gradual, one-step-at-a-time changes results in permanent healthy habits. Apply the turtle and the hare concept and you will come out ahead.

Because of today's emphasis on looking slim, the public is inundated with reducing diets. Rather than concentrating on how to lose weight, let's look at an optimal eating plan for maximizing your vitality and reducing your stress. This approach to food will also produce a thinner, healthier you.

When is the cornucopia of food not overflowing? At all occasions and celebrations the tables are heavily laden with food. Along with the typical three meals a day, there are the frequent office parties, birthdays, holiday spreads, picnics, cocktail parties, and television snacking. Do not forget the food served at tea parties, showers, bridge games, and football, basketball, and baseball games. Insufficient time is allowed for one meal to digest and assimilate before another morsel is stuffed into the mouth. The constant stream of social functions built around food challenges each one of us in our attempts to maintain a trim waistline and healthful diet.

One of the main causes of overeating is that food is more than a means to appease hunger or to enjoy a social function. Since childhood, we have been fed as a reward for doing well, or as an enticement to be good or quiet. For many, these beginnings have led to "feeding" a multitude of emotions. When frustrated or angry, disappointed or depressed, excited or bored, one quickly (and often subconsciously) reaches for the cookie jar, a candy bar, or a nibble from the refrigerator. In other words, we feel a positive or negative emotion in response to stress, and feed that emotion with distracted eating. The cause of the emotion does not change, but attention has been momentarily directed away from the problem, and one feels a temporary satisfaction and release through the act of eating.

## Unfortunately, four physiological stressors occur when feeding an emotion:

1. Thinking is less clear because blood is directed away from the brain and concentrated in the stomach;

2. The digestive process is less efficient because the parasympathetic nerves which stimulate digestion are slowed by feelings of anxiety and stress;

3. The process of assimilation is overtaxed by the amount of food and its mixed content; and

4. There is weight gain due to the type and amount of food eaten. In that emotional moment, usually sugar, chocolate, caffeine, rich pastries, or fast foods are absentmindedly gobbled.

To change these detrimental eating patterns, observe your thoughts. What thoughts and emotions are adversely influencing you to indulge in eating? The next time you find yourself unnecessarily (and often unwillingly) munching, note what it was that caused you to eat, and use the chart following. Some people reach for a cigarette or alcohol; frustrated eating is a similar response to stress.

## Changing Your Eating Responses to Stress

To attack what I call the stress/food syndrome, first familiarize yourself with how often and regularly you feed an emotion. Keep a diary or use the checklist below to catch yourself. Keep track until you see your patterns of emotional feeding. Discover which foods you feed to what emotions. This insight allows you to make conscious changes in your behavior. When I discovered the direct connection between anxiety and cookies, I was shocked by the consistency of the pattern. I reached for the cookie jar with every stress-producing situation. It was fascinating to observe myself. It then became amusing. The distancing created by observing myself, and not condemning myself, gradually led to a natural change in my behavior. Do not force a change. The observation in itself will lead to a response which is appropriate for you, especially if you decide to focus on positive changes towards balanced nutrition rather than trying to stop old, destructive patterns.

**ANXIETY AND COOKIES!**
When I discovered the direct connection between anxiety and cookies, I was shocked by the consistency of the pattern. I reached for the cookie jar with every stress-producing situation.

Example:

*anxiety/
cookies!*

## STRESS/FOOD SYNDROME PATTERNS

|  |  | MON | TUES | WED | THUR | FRI | SAT | SUN |
|---|---|---|---|---|---|---|---|---|
| **WEEK ONE** | Morning |  |  |  |  |  |  |  |
|  | Afternoon |  |  |  |  |  |  |  |
|  | Evening |  |  |  |  |  |  |  |
| **WEEK TWO** | Morning |  |  |  |  |  |  |  |
|  | Afternoon |  |  |  |  |  |  |  |
|  | Evening |  |  |  |  |  |  |  |
| **WEEK THREE** | Morning |  |  |  |  |  |  |  |
|  | Afternoon |  |  |  |  |  |  |  |
|  | Evening |  |  |  |  |  |  |  |
| **WEEK FOUR** | Morning |  |  |  |  |  |  |  |
|  | Afternoon |  |  |  |  |  |  |  |
|  | Evening |  |  |  |  |  |  |  |
| **WEEK FIVE** | Morning |  |  |  |  |  |  |  |
|  | Afternoon |  |  |  |  |  |  |  |
|  | Evening |  |  |  |  |  |  |  |

NOW THAT YOU SEE your stress/food syndrome patterns, supply your kitchen and office with healthy, easily available snacks which you can nibble. Juices and teas are an excellent choice. Often thirst is masked as hunger, and the need for more liquid is misinterpreted as a need for food. If you cannot break the habit of feeding your emotions, you can go a long way towards good health (and a slim figure) by consciously changing what you eat.

Use the stress/food syndrome checklist to notice what types of food you crave when you are stressed. The type of food is often related to the type of mood one is experiencing. When feeling bored or in need of nurturing, do you consume soft, creamy foods such as custards and pastries? When you are angry or frustrated, do you reach for chewy, hard foods such as nuts or popcorn? Replace these foods with nutritious, nonfat selections that are similar in texture to the foods that match your emotion. For example, keep crunchy celery, carrots, and apples on hand for biting into resentment or anxiety, and turn to nonfat, plain yogurt for lonely times.

Once you have adjusted to a change in what you eat, you can elect to go one step further: changing your response to stress. Rather than eating, engage in an activity that releases your tension.

## Examples of New Responses To Stress

◇ Take three, three-part rhythmic breaths.
◇ Go for a one-minute to twenty-minute walk.
◇ Do some slow, deep stretches.
◇ Close your eyes and affirm, "Peace *(strength, courage, love)* within brings peace *(strength, courage, love)* without."
◇ Jog in place.
◇ Tense and relax all your muscles three times.

AT FIRST YOU MAY FIND YOURSELF doing the stress-reducing technique and eating too. Observe the process, and then, just once, use discipline to stop yourself from eating. Use this one time as a starting point from which to drop the stress/food syndrome.

Before your next bout with the stress/food syndrome, practice several stress-releasing options that would be appropriate to your given situation and time frame. If the emotion is a low-energy emotion like depression, release the stress with an activity that gently raises your level of energy (for example, walking or stretching). Getting outside and breathing fresh air is helpful. If your stress is expressed as a high-energy emotion such as anger, do an initial active release such as *The Sun Salutation* (page 108) or jogging in place. Follow this with one of the calming techniques. Create your own new responses and practice them.

Visualization can be very helpful in this situation. Take time to sit and close your eyes. Take several breaths and then visualize a situation to which you previously responded by eating. Now replace that image. See yourself expressing a new, non-eating

response to stress. Practice this visualization several times a day and allow yourself to carry it out.

You are changing direction, turning yourself around from a life of anxiety to one of well-being. Initially this takes extra effort and preparation. Once you stop the downhill slide, the walk up the hill is expansive and more exhilarating with each step. You may backslide and find your hand in the cookie jar, but if you see the climb up as two steps forward, one step back, or as a zigzag, you will realize that the direction and momentum are still up. One backslide is not a change in direction, it just sets the pace of the upward climb.

The above comments and suggestions on diet and stress may not apply to you. Perhaps your challenge is to eat regularly. Rather than eating, you skip meals as a regular habit because of lack of time and lack of interest. Erratic eating is hard on your body and your health. As a general rule, it is better not to eat when you are emotionally wrought, because the food does not digest well, but at least start the day with a high-energy, nutritious breakfast.

I have discussed changing what you eat and/or substituting a stress-releasing skill as a response to your stressors. Perhaps you have tried this before, or it is not helpful for you. If so, try another approach. Rather than working on changing your response to your emotions, go back to the stress/food syndrome checklist and note the emotions you are experiencing. Look for perceptions you hold that are causing the emotions. Perhaps you can change your attitude to a situation or towards a person. Or is there anything you can do to change the situation itself? If you still cannot get to the root of the problem, perhaps the ideas below on compulsive eating will give you some ideas for positive change.

## Compulsive Eating

If you handle stress by compulsive eating, it may mean you are running away from facing your emotions by stuffing them down or suppressing them. Feeding a deep sense of lack produces a vicious cycle of overeating followed by sugar and fat cravings, which never result in fulfillment. Perhaps you are racing through life actively reaching outside yourself for happiness to avoid looking at a past trauma or a current pain. Keeping constantly busy, filling spare moments with eating, masks inner suffering.

Normally, eating as a response to stress results in overweight. The increasing bulge becomes an embarrassing sign of emotional turmoil. Weight due to compulsive eating becomes especially harmful when overeaters internalize the embarrassment of a pudgy body into a shame of their very existence. Whether or not low self-esteem initiated the eating response to stress, the resulting overweight usually leads to acute devaluation of the self.

Recently, I had the heartbreaking experience of witnessing this process. An obese client and I decided to sit in a sunny meadow for our counseling session. As we sat down, I adjusted my chair two

**EMOTIONS AND FOOD**
If you handle stress by compulsive eating, it may mean you are running away from facing your emotions by stuffing them down or suppressing them.

inches away from her because the uneven ground caused my chair to wobble. Her immediate reaction was to assume I moved back because I could not bear to be near her. Anger at herself for not being able to break her habit of overeating had become distorted into feelings of low self-worth and depression.

Authors John Bradshaw and Joan Borysenko state that there are two types of shame. Healthy shame results in taking responsibility for the outcome of a behavior and changing that behavior, or accepting the consequences of that behavior (overweight). Unhealthy shame results from turning an external act into an internal debasing of the self. According to Bradshaw, this process often begins in childhood. Devalued in childhood by conditional love and psychological abuse or neglect, the adult now carries a "wounded child within" who needs nurturing, not external feeding. Since 90% of American families are dysfunctional, most of us carry a "wounded child within." Our self-esteem and view of the world around us as friendly or unfriendly is largely a reflection of the degree of nurturing and unconditional love we received as children. [26,27]

Look at your past and search out possible unfulfilled needs of childhood. Perhaps compulsive eating today is a response to childhood abandonment, a feeding of childhood loss and loneliness. Changing eating patterns will not solve the problem because the roots are deeper. Past abuse, neglect, family alcoholism, and skewed family situations result in misconceptions about oneself and the universe. Often, past rejection by significant others has been internalized as lack of self-esteem and alienation from the surrounding world. This negative self-image may be expressed in dysfunctional eating patterns.

If this describes your situation, counseling or a support group may be needed to help you break the cycle of low self-esteem and compulsive eating. Apply the suggestions in this book, but if you need more support, do reach out for professional help.

One last suggestion for self-help is to take responsibility for fulfilling unmet childhood needs yourself. Rather than reaching out, expecting others to meet your needs, meet them yourself. You understand where you feel an inner lack and what is needed to fill the void. Nurture yourself with something other than food. Your "wounded child within" needs your love and parenting. The essence of who you are has been injured and needs your unconditional caring and support. The rewarding system suggested each week may help. It could be the most important part of the program for you if you make the weekly reward a fulfillment of the deepest need within you.

One client, after many years of unsuccessful relationships, saw that she was expecting her partners to make her happy. Rather than taking responsibility for her own happiness, she relied on her partners to fill the lonely void within. This pressure on her partners caused constant friction. With counseling, she began to accept herself, and to accept time when she was alone as a private healing

**THE WOUNDED CHILD WITHIN**
Look at your past and search out possible unfulfilled needs of childhood. Perhaps compulsive eating today is a response to childhood abandonment, a feeding of childhood loss and loneliness.

time, rather than as a time of remorse and proof that she was unworthy of being loved. As she gained her own independence and self-appreciation, she became a more loving, less demanding partner.

## Mood Foods

I have discussed the influence of moods on the choice of foods we eat. It is conversely true that we can influence our moods by what we eat. Specific foods can stimulate or calm us.

Foods containing an amino acid called tryptophan stimulate serotonin, which calms us and increases concentration. Foods containing the amino acid tyramine stimulate production of norepinephrine and dopamine, which give us a boost when we are fatigued. According to Judith Wurtman, author of *Managing Your Mind and Mood through Food*, this information translates into eating a small amount of protein to increase energy and alertness and a small amount of carbohydrates as a natural tranquilizer.

Choose low-fat, protein-rich foods to increase motivation, reaction time, and alertness. When you have plans for a busy afternoon, or need an extra boost to finish the day's projects, eat a lunch high in protein or have a late afternoon snack of no more than 3-4 ounces of lean beef, skinned chicken, fish, or a low-fat dairy product. Before bedtime, Wurtman suggests a carbohydrate (sweet or starch) to induce a sleepy, relaxed mood. Warm food, such as tea with sugar or honey, or a warm muffin, not only provides the carbohydrate, but also gives a sense of nurturing and security. Have no more than 1-2 ounces of the carbohydrate for the desired effect, and to prevent weight gain, make low-fat selections. For those 20% or more over their ideal weight or for women a few days prior to menstruation, 2-3 ounces may be required.

**THE POWER LUNCH**
When you have plans for a busy afternoon, or need an extra boost to finish the day's projects, eat a lunch high in protein or have a late afternoon snack.

## The Stress Management Diet

Moderation is the building block of sound nutrition and a stress-free diet. Irregular eating patterns, pendulum swings from starvation to binging, and constant overeating disrupt health and stability. Dr. Peter Van Houten, director of the Sierra Family Medical Center in Nevada City, California, recommends moderation as the most effective approach to sound nutrition. He says it is what you eat day-to-day that is important, not the Friday night heavy meal or the once-a-week rich dessert. He argues that restricted diets take the pleasure and relaxation out of eating. He encourages his patients to eat with awareness, to watch calories, salt, fat, and cholesterol intake without the stress of complete denial. Stress-free eating means observing daily patterns and making minimal but consistent changes towards healthy nutrition. To avoid the mental and emotional stress connected with pendulum swings from restriction to excess, first become aware of your eating habits without changing them, and observe the physical, mental, and emotional effects of your current diet. The most effective way to change the unhealthy aspects of your diet is to see change as directional and to view it within the framework of long rhythms. To avoid stress, remember that the process of working toward an ideal is more important than the goal itself. Do not set restrictions to be endured for a specific amount of time; instead make incremental changes within the framework of a lifetime direction of healthy eating.

There is no diet that is right for everyone, and it only creates stress to follow someone else's ideal diet. Dieting in itself is stressful because of the built-in nature of an outside authority dictating what you eat. Balance enjoyment with healthful eating and observe nutritional habits which work for you. Changes do not happen overnight. It takes time and listening to your body to learn its nutritional requirements. Consult a nutritional practitioner if you are not sure how to correct an imbalance in your system.

## Nutritional Tips for Reducing Stress

If you have a highly stressful lifestyle, following one or more of the following suggestions will enhance your vitality and reduce your stress symptomology. For those who relieve stress through overeating, they will also help you to reduce weight.

1. Eat more fruits and vegetables. A salad once a day is excellent for your health. Raw salads are not only rich in vital nutrients, but give you fiber to help in elimination. Green leafy vegetables are an excellent source of calcium, which the body demands when under stress.

2. Eat as much fresh food as you can. The more processed the food, the less vitality available to you. A bowl of fresh fruit is as easy to prepare as a bowl of canned fruit and much better for you. If your tension expresses itself as indigestion, light meals with emphasis on fruit alone or vegetables (do not eat them at the same meal) can work wonders. If you have trouble digesting raw foods, lightly steam or bake them. Add a little water to sliced fruit such as apples, bananas, and pears and simmer for a warm, easy-to-digest breakfast on a cold, winter day.

**STRESS AND NUTRIENTS**
Stress robs your body of nutrients, especially the B vitamins, which are called the anti-stress vitamins.

3. Begin to shift from demineralized cereals, white flour, and white rice to whole grain breads and grains. Stress robs your body of nutrients, especially the B vitamins, which are called the anti-stress vitamins. Whole grains and breads are rich in these important vitamins. Nutritional yeast is an excellent source of B vitamins and can be sprinkled in soups (homemade, if possible) or on salads, or added to casseroles. If you are allergic to wheat, try some of the delicious sprouted breads which have no wheat in them, or bread made with corn.

4. When you're under stress, your immune system is weakened. Vitamin C is essential for proper functioning of the adrenal and thyroid glands and "promotes healing in every condition of ill health." [28] Good sources of vitamin C are citrus fruits and juices and all fresh fruits and vegetables, especially broccoli, tomatoes, green

bell peppers, apples, and kiwis. Eat some of these daily or have a large raw salad.

5. Avoid sugar, by the teaspoon or hidden in processed foods. For example, there are eight tablespoons of sugar in a twelve-ounce serving of Pepsi or Coca-Cola. In terms of stress management, sugar gives you an initial burst of energy, but is followed by a low-energy, depressed feeling, because it upsets the balance in your blood sugar level.

6. Avoid or cut down on caffeine in coffee, black teas, soft drinks, and chocolate. Caffeine draws the B vitamins out of the body. After the initial stimulus, there is a reduction of energy. Ask anyone who has given up coffee and he will tell you he has more energy and has less of the pendulum swing of energy to lethargy.

Reduce the amount of coffee you drink, or mix it half and half with decaffeinated coffee; or, if possible, give it up entirely. You will be surprised how much better you feel. I drank one cup of coffee a day for a year. At about 4 p.m. every day I was exhausted. I now maintain as full a schedule as before and I am tired at the end of the day; but it is a natural tiredness, not the exhaustion I felt before quitting my one cup of coffee.

7. Eat three meals a day. This is essential. Stress is exacerbated by irregular eating patterns.

8. Make rich meals and desserts a treat rather than a daily habit. Have a small piece of lasagna or chocolate mousse, but then keep the next meal light, with an emphasis on fiber.

9. A general rule is to eat those foods that give you energy yet do not tax the system. The answer lies in eating fresh, live foods in correct combination so as to aid digestion, assimilation, and elimination.

Nutrition is as controversial as politics and religion, with countless books and theories on what is healthy. For stress management, the above tips are guidelines. The essential rules are moderation, common sense, and a diet that is both enjoyable and healthy for you.

If you want to delve into another approach, on the following page is a healthful, highly disciplined diet which has had success in battling illness, in aiding in stress reduction, and for weight loss. Consult with your physician before making any significant changes in your nutritional patterns. This more stringent regimen has been very beneficial for some people, but it may not be best for you. It is a low-fat (optimally less than 20%) vegetarian diet with emphasis on fresh (organic, if possible) foods. This diet has no fish, chicken, or red meat, no eggs, and only low-fat dairy products. It includes only those foods listed on the following page.

**STIMULANTS CAN INCREASE STRESS**
Avoid or cut down on caffeine in coffee, black teas, soft drinks, and chocolate....After the initial stimulus, there is a reduction of energy.

## A Healthful, Highly Disciplined, Low-Fat Diet

◇ Fresh fruits and vegetables (*70% of your diet*)
◇ Whole grains: *especially brown rice, oats, millet, and buckwheat*
◇ Legumes: *best sprouted to increase vitamin and mineral content*
◇ Dairy products: *focus on low-fat milk and yogurt, and soft cheeses or the new low-fat hard cheeses*
◇ Herbal teas *such as peppermint, chamomile, and lemon verbena*
◇ Honey or fruit juices *for sweetening, rather than sugar*
◇ Fresh fruit and vegetable juices

TO MAINTAIN SUCH A DIET, eat hearty meals that emphasize the food itself rather than the condiments under which the food is usually buried. For example, to keep to the low-fat aspect of the diet, use one of the no-oil salad dressings on the market or create your own. I use a little vinegar and vegetable broth with brewer's yeast. Or you could use a squeeze of lemon, mashed avocado, and herbs. Skip the butter on vegetables, including corn and potatoes, or use a little of the monosaturated oils such as olive oil. To keep the fat down, do not use mayonnaise in sandwiches; instead, try the following nonfat yogurt spread. Take several tablespoons of nonfat plain yogurt and place it in the refrigerator overnight in a strainer covered with cheesecloth, or in a coffee filter paper or a paper towel. The next morning toss away the drained liquid collected in the pan below the strainer and flavor the resulting yogurt spread with your favorite spices. I use this on potatoes and sometimes in salads. Use egg substitute or egg whites in your baking. If you are new to vegetarianism, ask your local health food store for a good cookbook. Foreign cuisines, such as Chinese, Mexican, and Italian, have many non-meat entrees which are easy to prepare. I have been a vegetarian for over twenty years and highly recommend that you give it a try for stress reduction and healthy living.

This low-fat vegetarian diet can be tailored to fit what you and your physician feel is best for you. The American Cancer Society and the American Heart Association recommend a low-fat diet (maximum 30% fat) and cutting back on red meat be-

## HOW MUCH FAT IS IN THE FOODS YOU EAT?

**IT ISN'T HARD TO FIGURE OUT** how much fat is in the foods we eat. But it's almost impossible just by looking at the label! Often, the fat content is listed in grams or milligrams. But what you need to know is "What percentage of the calories in this food come from fat?" The simple mathematical formula in this chart will help you to watch out for your fat consumption.

### STEP ONE

| Grams of Fat | X | 9 | = | Calories from Fat |
|---|---|---|---|---|
| (Per serving) | | (Calories/gram) | | (Per serving) |

### STEP TWO

| Calories from Fat | ÷ | Total Calories | = | Percentage of Fat |
|---|---|---|---|---|
| (Per serving) | | (Per serving) | | (In food) |

**FOR EXAMPLE:** In whole milk, the label lists 8 gm of fat per serving. Times that by 9 and you get 72 calories from fat per serving. Divine that by 150 (the total calories per serving) and you get 48%. **In short, 48% of the calories in whole milk come from fat!**

cause of it's high cholesterol They say you should eat a maximum 300 mg. of cholesterol per day. If you do not know the percentage of fat in a food you are eating, the following will help you. Find the percentage of fat in a product by multiplying the number of grams of fat by nine and then dividing the result by the total calories. The number of calories and amount of fat are listed on packaged food. A general rule of thumb for controlling cholesterol intake is to avoid saturated fats and reduce consumption of animal products such as red meat and dairy products, including butter and eggs.

## Food Combining

Another focus in vegetarianism is to concentrate on proper food combining to obtain all the amino acids (components of a complete protein) and to maximize absorption of vitamins, minerals, and other nutrients. The following are guidelines for correct food combining:

1. Do not eat fruits and vegetables together. It is best to eat fruit alone. Breakfast is the optimal time to have fruit, or eat it alone as a snack.

2. When you are eating flesh foods, combine the fish, chicken, or meat with salad or vegetables, but do not eat carbohydrates such as grains and pasta at the same meal as the protein.

3. Combine carbohydrates with vegetables, cooked or raw. For more information and detail on food combining read *Fit for Life* by H. and M. Diamond. [29] For more information on the effects of processed foods on a stressed system read *Prescription for Life* by Dr. Edward Taub. [30]

4. If you are observing a diet which has little or no meat or dairy, be sure to get complete proteins. During the digestive process, proteins are broken down into 22 amino acids. Eight of these amino acids (called "essential" amino acids) cannot be produced within your system and must be obtained from

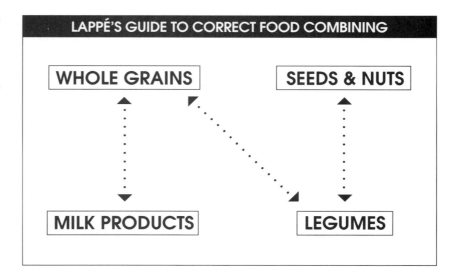

food. To obtain the complete protein, it is necessary to eat foods in combination so that the essential amino acids lacking in one food are supplied by another food. It is a relatively simple task to be sure to eat these complementing proteins within the same meal or with the next one. (For more information on food combining for complete proteins see *Diet for a Small Planet Revisited* by Francis Lappé.) Pictured here is Lappé's food guide for correct combining for complete proteins. [31]

The dashed lines indicate that several items in each group complement one another. If there is no connecting line, you can eat

the foods together, but only a few items in eacl
one another for the complete protein. Exam
foods to get all eight essential amino acids t
protein are: eating rice and beans (grain and
yogurt and granola (milk product and grain).

Let me again emphasize that nutrition ca
role in reducing stress only if it is carried out w
enthusiasm. Take your first steps with a suggest
lesson, and gradually make changes only whei
enjoy the results.

# INSTANT STRESS RELEASER

## Guidelines for Long-Range Stress Management

Stress is the spice of life. Successful stress management is not
running away from stress. It is saying YES to health and well-being,
while exploring life's challenges and fulfilling your highest
potential. All of us are seeking happiness. The deepest joy comes
from within and is expressed outwardly in loving life, loving your
family, friends, and yourself, and finding meaning in your work and
relationships.

The *joie de vivre* is lost when we rush through every experience and miss the present moment. We lose the essence of life by
filling it with guilt or worry over the past, or filling it with plans for
the future. In all the rush, we miss the ever-present NOW.

Stress management is opening your heart, your mind, and your
will to live, without losing the balance of inner calm and peace. We
need to prioritize our lives, so that in striving for success, we leave
room for introspection and personal, creative expression. We need
to allow space in our days for relaxing, stretching, and letting go of
tension. If we can balance our lives in this way, we will be more
productive, more efficient, healthier, and happier.

*The Fitness Option* has given you tools for stress reduction and
the means to apply these tools to your life in a way that is not time-
consuming. For continued success in controlling stress, create a
program of your own. Continue using the exercises, breathing,
quiet time techniques, and instant stress releasers, and add your own
options to fit your special needs.

Which of the exercises and techniques worked best for
you? Do you want to investigate more of the physical stretching? If
so, turn to the second chapter in *Part III*, which has additional exercises for releasing tension through more advanced physical
exercises. Or use the information in the first chapter of *Part III* if you
enjoy stretching but have lower back problems. A healthy, elastic
spine keeps you youthful and healthy. When the spine is in correct
alignment, the nerves coming out of the spine between the vertebrae
are not pinched. The organs, glands, and muscles fed by these

nerves function optimally. Perhaps the quiet time techniques were most helpful for you. Make a tape of you talking yourself through the relaxation sequence, or use my audio tape, *Relaxations,* which has five ten-minute relaxations/guided meditations on it, and is available through the La Jolla Institute For Stress Management. (See the last page of this book for more information.)

You may want to continue exploration and practice of the instant stress releasers. These perceptual exercises increase your ability to reduce mental anxiety and physical tension.

Aerobic exercise, whether it be biking, walking briskly, swimming, aerobics classes, jogging, or enjoying a sport of your choice, is healthy for your cardiovascular system and excellent for stress management. Tight muscles are relaxed, circulation is increased, and mood-elevating hormones are released into the system.

Use your own creative resources and understanding of yourself to put together a fitness option program that will be long lasting because it is both enjoyable and beneficial to you. For example, a close friend balances her intense work schedule and numerous business trips with running, meditation, and jigsaw puzzles. She finds that an hour concentrating on sorting out the pieces clears her mind and is very relaxing. In today's world we have little time that is not structured. Even while driving, some people shave, cram down a sandwich, or conduct a conference call on the car phone. For your fitness option, take into account the need for unstructured time where you do something of your own choosing.

Time is *of the essence* in stress reduction. Managing your time well can instantly reduce your level of stress.

◇ Organize your day or week with a written list.
◇ Prioritize your commitments.
◇ Delegate responsibilities and tasks if possible.
◇ Leave some tasks undone if completion means
    overtaxing yourself.
◇ Allow time for relaxation and enjoyment. Balanced living
    saves you time in the long run.

IF YOU FEEL PRESSURED BY LACK OF TIME to do the routines in this program, take only as much time as feels comfortable and beneficial to you. Choose your favorite exercises and focus on the breathing and perceptual exercises. Or use the guidelines below for the time-saving method for stress management.

# INTEGRATING STRESS MANAGEMENT SKILLS INTO YOUR LIFE

THE FOLLOWING IS A REVIEW/REMINDER of how to make the practice of stress management skills a part of your lifestyle.

## Stretching

Continue integrating the relaxation skills of stretching, breathing, deep relaxation, and quiet time into your daily activities. As you began in *Week One,* insert the relaxation skills of the program into other activities.

Have you been stretching at the office, in the car, during simple tasks, or while watching television? When at a desk have you taken stress breaks at regular intervals to do the exercises for tense shoulders and neck? This small habit will break the build-up of chronic tension and, through improved circulation, keep you more alert. Do a few of the exercises *before* there is a build-up of tension. While driving, have you made it a habit to do some *Neck Rolls* and *Shoulder Shrugs* at a red light? Do a few stretches as you are dressing, or after every shower use a towel as a strap to do the *Standing Shoulder Stretch.* Do the *Full Body Stretch* at the kitchen sink or at your office desk if appropriate. While talking on the home telephone, stand and stretch your hamstrings, rotate your spine, or lie on your back and do the wall exercises. While walking do the *Chest Expander.* Before getting out of bed bring each knee to the chest and then do one of the twists on your back. Make these and stretches of your own a regular practice and it will take no time out of your busy schedule while preventing a build-up of muscular tension.

## Breathing

Breathing exercises are even easier to fit into your daily routine. Have you been practicing slow *Diaphragmatic Breaths,* the *Complete Breath,* or the *Three-Part Rhythmic Breath* each time you have found your-self waiting? Breathing consciously will bring you into a calmer frame of mind and oxygenate your brain and body. If you feel listless or depressed, take three *Complete Breaths* followed by three *Double Breaths,* or do three rounds of the *Bellows Breath.*

According to John Mason, author of *Guide to Stress Reduction,* a businessman decided to take one *Complete Breath* each time he looked at his watch. He discovered that in one day he took over fifty *Complete Breaths.* After less than two weeks a fellow worker asked if he were on medication, because his personality had changed so much for the better. [23] Practice conscious breathing. You and those around you will benefit!

When you are experiencing anxiety, remember to breathe slowly and deeply. Our breathing reflects our state of mind. Help

break the biofeedback loop between the body and the mind by consciously changing your breathing pattern. Continue with the slow, deep breathing until you feel more relaxed.

## Deep Relaxation

Deep relaxation is one stress management skill you may wish to continue enjoying in its full form. At the end of the day, stretch out, play some soothing music, and go through one of the deep relaxation techniques. If you have insomnia, practice just before going to sleep or when you awake in the middle of the night. You will wake up more refreshed.

     If you do not have time for the ten-minute deep relaxations, take a half-a-minute to relax from your head to your feet at times throughout the day. You have learned how to consciously relax your muscles and what situations give rise to your stress symptomology. If it is difficult to relax the muscles, actively tense and relax your large muscle groups from your feet to your head.

     Do not be fooled by the simplicity of the techniques. You can, with a little perseverance, make small changes in habit that will make large differences in your level of experienced stress.

**MINI-DEEP RELAXATIONS**
If you do not have time for the ten-minute deep relaxations, take a half-a-minute to relax from your head to your feet at times throughout the day.

## Attitude

Continue to observe your thoughts and their emotional and physical expression. Remember the basic tenet of stress reduction: *You* decide how you see yourself and those around you. Are you still expressing negative self-talk? Do you hear yourself making statements that indicate uncertainty and a lack of self-confidence? Are your expectations of yourself unrealistic? Reread the instant stress releaser section in *Week Four* if you need a refresher on how to deal with negative thought patterns about yourself or your circumstances. You can moderate "type A" behavior by changing your perspective.

## Meditation and Creative Quiet Time

*Meditative Deep Relaxation* or your own creative quiet time may need to become a part of your daily activity. Sitting down in a quiet setting, and observing your breath and relaxing on the exhalation is medically recognized for its ability to elicit the relaxation response. If this does not fit your time frame or interest, be creative. The key is to spend a minimum of ten minutes a day, attention focused in the present moment, on something you enjoy that is not work-related.

## Creative Quiet Time Examples:

     1. If you run or do any other form of aerobic activity, concentrate in the present, on the activity itself, the surrounding environment, or your breath. Aerobic exercise releases a mood-

elevating hormone in the brain, increases circulation to tired muscles, and is excellent for the heart and weight reduction. Adding a mental focus to aerobic activities increases their benefits in reducing tension.

2. Integrate creative quiet time into a commonplace activity, such as taking a shower, eating a meal, or commuting to work. During that time take a conscious break from subjects that create stress for you. Attend to the detail of what you are doing. Apply the same discipline as with the other techniques. Say "time out" to stress; concentrate on the present activity. Enjoy the shower, the meal, or the commute.

3. In a similar vein, if you have the time, take a walk in a beautiful setting such as a park or the beach, and observe all the sights around you. Become aware of the colors and shapes about you. Keep this focus for ten minutes. The next time either repeat, or concentrate on all the sounds around you. The third time pay attention to how your body moves and feels.

If the only time you are walking is between appointments, reduce your stress by practicing concentration in the present as you walk. You could make it a habit to do the focusing exercise every time you park your car, even if it is only a few steps to your destination.

4. Sit or lie down and choose an abstract subject for your focus. You might choose the topic of peace, courage, or love. Direct the mind to stay with the chosen topic for ten minutes. If you concentrate/contemplate daily on a specific quality, by the end of a week you will begin to express that quality in your activities. Hold to the same subject for weeks, and even months, and you will understand and experience deeper levels of this chosen quality or attitude. Initially you are analyzing the quality in a subject/object relationship. As your concentration deepens, that quality within you begins to flower and grow. A part of yourself, as yet untapped, is vitalized and strengthened by the contemplation.

One means of intensifying your experience of the quality is "breathing" it. As you inhale, mentally draw the quality into yourself with the breath. As you exhale, visualize the quality flooding your mind, your emotions, and your body. Let the peace and calmness fill all parts of your being. Stay with the breathing of the quality until you begin to experience the effect: Feel how it has changed the rhythm and depth of your breath, how it has reduced the level of tension in your muscles, and how it has affected the state of your mind. An indication of progress is to begin to see the effects of meditation/creative quiet time outside of the practice itself. If your focus was peace, has your daily concentration on peace resulted in a calmer you?

You control your attitude, and your body reflects your choice. You can view the challenges of your life as opportunities for growth or as obstacles. The choice is yours; the results are yours.

5. Admittedly, creative quiet time takes time out of your schedule, but perhaps your stress is a result of not taking time for

**"BREATHING-IN" A QUALITY**
One means of intensifying your experience of the quality is "breathing" it. As you inhale, mentally draw the quality into yourself with the breath.

personal relaxation and creative self-expression. Enjoy a new sport or hobby that you have not given yourself permission to do. While engaged in this activity, enjoy it in detail, in the present moment. This is not lost time. You will return to your job, duty, or demanding situation with a refreshed, clear mind and a relaxed body. A conscious break from the demands of life increases rather than decreases productivity. The only stipulation is to choose something you enjoy and to do it with your full attention.

6. If you are with other people who are needlessly dwelling on a stressful subject, change the subject or direct the conversation to what is happening around you, to the activity itself, or to the surrounding environment.

7. Do not forget to reward yourself this week and always. You deserve it!

**TAKE BREAKS!**
A conscious break from the demands of life increases rather than decreases productivity.

## *BREATHING EXERCISE*

### Bellows Breath

The *Bellows Breath* is stimulating. It revitalizes the body and clears the mind. It strengthens the diaphragm and abdominal muscles, gives a wonderful internal massage, and helps to normalize digestion. The action of the diaphragm stimulates the stomach, spleen, liver, and pancreas and aids in normalizing their functions. It is a beneficial technique for those with asthma.

To practice the *Bellows Breath,* remain on your back and place the soles of your feet close to your buttocks on the carpet. Close your eyes and focus your attention in the abdominal area. Because learning the *Bellows Breath* assumes the ability to breathe diaphragmatically, observe your natural breathing to be sure you are relaxing the abdominal muscles as you inhale and contracting them as you exhale. The *Bellows Breath* is similar, but done more rapidly and vigorously, with emphasis on the exhalation. Breathe through the nose throughout the exercise, strongly contracting your abdominal muscles on the exhalation. Keep the inhalation and the exhalation short and equal in length, pumping the lungs like a bellows.

Practice with your hand over your navel to be sure you are contracting the abdominal muscles on the exhalation. You will feel a warmth in the abdominal area from exerting the muscles. Now that you have the feel of accentuating the exhalation, do not focus on the length of either breath. Keep both the inhalation and the exhalation active and strong. Take your time to learn it properly to maximize the benefits. Practice a set of four to six breaths at a time, gradually building up to ten breaths. Follow a set with one *Three-Part Rhythmic Breath*. Repeat the whole exercise with a round of the *Bellows Breath* and the *Three-Part Rhythmic Breath* two more times. Once you can do the exercise correctly, practice three rounds in a sitting position.

# WEEK FIVE ROUTINE

Complete Breath
Bellows Breath
The Cat
The Inverted V
Sitting Stretch
Standing Shoulder Stretch
Palm Press and Sway
Extended Forward Bend
Seated Lumbar Twist
The Fish
Lower Back Stretch
Meditative Deep Relaxation: Labeling Your Thoughts

READ THE DETAILED DISCUSSION of the week's exercises, and then use the At-A-Glance section as a reference.

# DETAILED INSTRUCTIONS ON WEEK FIVE EXERCISES

### The Complete Breath
Stretch out on your back, and take a minute to let your attention come into your muscles. Be aware of how they feel and then relax them. With your eyes closed take three *Complete Breaths,* filling the lungs from bottom to top and exhaling in the opposite direction. Repeat two more times. With each exhalation let go of residual physical and mental tension.

### Bellows Breath
Practice three rounds of the *Bellows Breath* (this week's breathing exercise) on your back and then three more rounds sitting up. Practice only one round if you feel dizzy. Build up slowly to more rounds.

### The Cat
Practice *The Cat* exercise again this week, as described in detail in *Week One* (page 28).

The Inverted V (First Position)

The Inverted V (Second Position)

The Inverted V (Third Position)

## The Inverted V

**First Position:** Remain in *The Cat* position, curl your toes under, and push your buttocks toward the ceiling by straightening your legs. Stay high on your toes and stretch through your shoulders by pressing your chest toward your thighs. Relax your neck, press evenly into your palms, thumbs, and little and middle fingers. Feel as if you were hanging from the ceiling by your buttocks.

 **Second Position:** Holding the first position, begin alternately stretching the calves by bicycling the legs. Straighten the right knee and push the right heel toward the floor while bending the left knee and keeping on the ball of the left foot. Alternate, stretching each leg three times.

 **Third Position:** Now lift high on the balls of both feet as in the first position, and then very gently lower the heels towards the floor. Hold for three breaths, stretching through the arms, relaxing the neck, and pressing the heels down and the buttocks up. Come back down into *The Cat* to finish.

## Sitting Stretch

Sit on the edge of a pillow in a cross-legged position, place your left hand on your left knee, and twist to face the right knee. Push your left hand against your knee to help you assume this position. Inhale and stretch the spine into a correct upright position. Exhale and bend from the hips over the right knee. Place your hands on each side of the right knee on the carpet to help keep the chest open. Take three *Diaphragmatic Breaths.* Inhale and come back into the upright sitting position. Repeat to the other side.

Sitting Stretch

Standing Shoulder Stretch

## Standing Shoulder Stretch

Take a towel, strap, or belt and hold one end in each hand with the strap in front of you. While maintaining correct posture, bring your arms over your head and then slowly behind you to shoulder height. At this point you will feel a stretch in the chest. If there is too much of a stretch, place your hands further apart on the strap. If you do not feel a stretch, bring your hands closer together on the strap. Bring your arms in a wide arc in front again. Repeat from front to back and back to front again. Practice two more times.

Palm Press and Sway

## Palm Press and Sway

First practice the *Palm Press* as taught in *Week One*. Lower your arms to complete the exercise. Take a *Complete Breath*. Maintain correct standing posture, with the feet parallel and one inch apart.

Come back into the *Palm Press* position. Keeping the palms together, tucking the pelvis, and tightening the buttocks and abdominal muscles, inhale and stretch up through the trunk of your body. As you exhale, bend to the left and let the hips go to the right. Stretch through the arms as you bend to the side, but keep the neck elongated by pulling down the shoulder and upper back muscles. Continue to keep the lower back flat, with the abdominals tight to protect the lower back. Take three *Diaphragmatic Breaths* in this position. Inhale as you come back into an upright position. Repeat to the other side.

## Extended Forward Bend

As taught in the first week, bend forward in *The Rag Doll* with the trunk curled and the knees bent two inches or more. Come down as far as you can and then shake your neck and shoulders to relax them. Take three *Diaphragmatic Breaths* in this position. On the next inhalation, take hold of your big toes, ankles, or shins and straighten your arms, lifting the trunk of your body away from your legs. Open the chest, lengthen the neck, and push the buttocks toward the ceiling. As you exhale, bring the trunk again towards the knees with the top of the head extending towards the floor. Repeat the extension away from the knees and back toward the floor two more times. Come into a standing position by bending the knees two or more inches and rolling up with a curled spine. In the standing position, keep the chin tucked for a breath to prevent dizziness.

Extended Forward Bend

## Seated Lumbar Twist

**First Position:** This stretch is excellent for maintaining elasticity in the lumbar spine and releasing tension. Start in a seated position on the edge of a pillow with both legs straight in front of you. Bend your left knee and place the sole of your foot as close to your body as you can. Wrap the crook of your right elbow around the knee. Put your left hand on the carpet behind you close to your buttocks. As you inhale, press your left hand against the carpet to facilitate correct spinal alignment. As you exhale, press your forearm against your left knee to increase the rotation of your spine. While maintaining the position, flex the heel of the right foot and keep your chin parallel to the carpet and your shoulders rolled back and down. Take two more breaths in this position. Repeat to the other side.

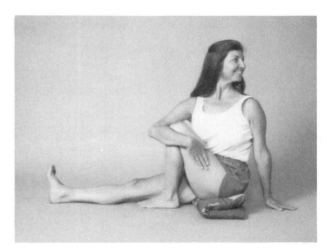

Seated Lumbar Twist (First Position)

**Advanced Position:** If you have the flexibility, rather than crooking the elbow around the opposite knee, bring your upper arm to the outside of your leg and rest your lower arm and hand on your thigh, or place your right hand around the arch of your left foot. This increases the stretch.

Keep this a gentle stretch. Do not overdo; relax into the rotation and keep pushing against the carpet to keep the spine from slouching. To increase stretch in the intercostal muscles between the ribs, and to rotate further, use *Three-Part Rhythmic Breathing* while holding the position.

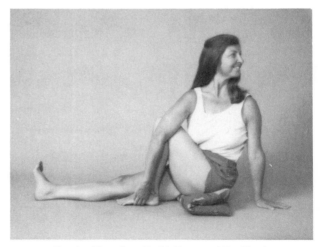

Seated Lumbar Twist (Second Position)

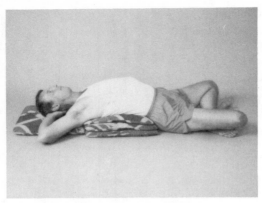

The Fish (First Position)

The Fish (Second Position)

The Fish (Third Position)

## The Fish

This exercise is excellent for releasing tension in the upper back, neck, and shoulders and stretches out tension along the front of the torso. Practicing the *Complete Breath* in this position helps relieve tightness in the chest. Practice all variations of this stretch with the legs either stretched out straight or cross-legged, whichever is more comfortable.

**First Position:** Start in a seated position with a pillow (or folded blanket) behind your hips. Do not sit on the pillow. Clasp your fingers behind your head. Tightening your abdominal muscles, curl your spine, and slowly lower your back over the pillow and then arch back. Keep your chin tucked and stretch the back of your neck by using a smaller pillow under the head or making your hands into fists, one on top of the other, and resting your head on the top fist. Gently press the elbows toward the floor and enjoy the stretch.

For a gentler stretch through the chest and shoulders use a sofa cushion or pillow large enough for your head and arms to remain on the pillow. Adjust pillow size or blanket height to make the stretch comfortable and relaxing. Take six *Complete Breaths* in this position.

**Second Position:** If you would like more of an arch in the position and you have no neck problems, do not use a blanket or pillow. Place your hands (palms down) under your buttocks. Press on your elbows and lift the chest so that you come onto the top of your head. Take three *Complete Breaths* in this position.

**Third Position:** For more of an arch, hold the second position for only one breath and then press on your elbows so that your head comes off the floor. Bring your elbows closer together. Take three more breaths in this position. To come out of the stretch separate your elbows, lower onto the top of your head, and ease out of the position; or if your neck is strong enough, lift your head and look toward your feet and lower your spine to the floor by tucking your hips, then curling your chest, and lastly tucking your chin and lowering your head to the carpet.

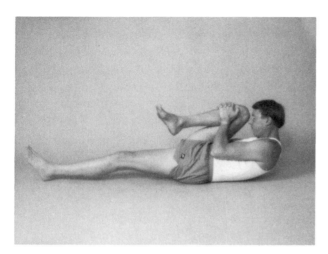
Lower Back Stretch

## Lower Back Stretch

Upon completion of *The Fish,* bring your left knee to your chest and clasp your hands around your shin. Bring your head toward your bent knee. Tighten your abdominal muscles and take three breaths in this position. Do not scrunch your shoulders. Repeat with the other leg. Practice the exercise one more time to each side.

# DEEP RELAXATION

## Meditative Deep Relaxation: Labeling Your Thoughts

Begin in a comfortable seated position or in the deep relaxation position, with pillows under your thighs if needed. Start with three *Double Breaths,* increasing the tension on each inhalation and relaxing more deeply with each exhalation. Next take three, *Three-Part Rhythmic Breaths,* quieting the body and the mind with each exhalation.

Allow your awareness to be in the present, silently mindful and attentive to the experience of the moment. Each time you have a thought, observe it, and then label it. For example, label it a "worrying," "planning," "daydreaming," or "rehearsing" thought. After you have labeled it, let the thought go out of the consciousness. When the next thought bubbles up to the surface of your mind, repeat the observing/labeling/releasing process. As you practice, fewer and fewer thoughts will arise. You will experience a deep sense of inner quiet and harmony, a cessation from the noise of your thoughts.

# REWARDING YOURSELF

HOPEFULLY, BY THE FIFTH WEEK of the program you have made some aspect of the program your own. Perhaps it is the aspect of rewarding yourself. In taking responsibility for your well-being, you need to include enjoyment and relaxation as an essential element of your fitness program. Our lives need this balance to allow full expression of not only what we can *do,* but who we *are.*

# WEEKLY REVIEW

## Lesson Summary
Part of stress management is eating sensibly, particularly eating fresh fruits and vegetables, whole grains and legumes, and foods low in fat, cholesterol, and sugar. Eat three regular meals a day and try not to eat after dinner. These simple rules will stabilize your blood sugar, reduce your weight, and help you cope with stress. If you are feeding your emotions rather than your hunger, gradually change what you eat from processed, fat- and sugar-laden foods to satisfying, healthy foods. Next, attempt to change your response to stress from one of eating to an alternative stress-reducing activity. Above all, the process of changing nutritional habits needs to be in gradual steps, with an eye to moderation.

# CHARTING YOUR PROGRESS

| MON | TUES | WED | THUR | FRI | SAT | SUN | RELAXATION SKILL |
|-----|------|-----|------|-----|-----|-----|------------------|
| ☐ | ☐ | ☐ | ☐ | ☐ | ☐ | ☐ | BREATHING EXERCISES |
| ☐ | ☐ | ☐ | ☐ | ☐ | ☐ | ☐ | PHYSICAL EXERCISES |
| ☐ | ☐ | ☐ | ☐ | ☐ | ☐ | ☐ | DEEP RELAXATION |
| ☐ | ☐ | ☐ | ☐ | ☐ | ☐ | ☐ | INSTANT STRESS RELEASER |
| ☐ | ☐ | ☐ | ☐ | ☐ | ☐ | ☐ | OTHER STRESS-REDUCING ACTIVITY (Jogging, listening to calming music, etc.) |
| ☐ | ☐ | ☐ | ☐ | ☐ | ☐ | ☐ | LEVEL OF STRESS (Rate on a scale of 1-10) |

**Directions:** Place an X after each relaxation skill you practiced for that day. Evaluate your stress level at the end of each day on a scale of 1-10, with 10 representing a high level of stress. Review at the end of the week and note which techniques have been the most beneficial for you.

1) The Cat (In Four Positions)

2) The Inverted V (In Three Positions)

3) Sitting Stretch

4) Standing Shoulder Stretch

5) Palm Press and Sway (First Position)

5) Palm Press and Sway (Second Position)

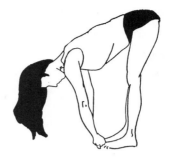

6) Extended Forward Bend (In Two Positions)

7) Seated Lumbar Twist
(With Advanced Position)

8) The Fish (In Three Positions)

9) Lower Back Stretch

10) Meditative Deep Relaxation: Labeling Your Thoughts
(With Alternate Position)

# FIVE-WEEK FITNESS OPTION PROGRAM SUMMARY

## Conclusion

*You have completed* Part Two *of the five-week* Fitness Option Program *to healing stress. You now have tools for managing your tension. You have learned mini-stretching routines, conscious breathing exercises, instant deep relaxations, and creative quiet time to enable you to change your experience of life, making it fuller and richer. You also have learned the skills of observation and of living in the present moment. You now know to be aware of your thought patterns and stress symptomology and how to change your perceptions and alleviate your tensions. This stress management program, with your creative applications, can be transforming. It is your responsibility and challenge to practice the skills, to be creative with them, and to enjoy them. Make it an exhilarating journey. It can have its setbacks and trials, but remember the longer rhythm. The path of change is challenging and the rewards dramatic.*

You *are the sculptor of your life. Express your full potential and feel the joy of that creation!*

BEFORE GOING ON TO PART III, *retake the stress tests you took at the beginning of the course (at the end of the introductory chapter). Take them now, before looking at how you did five weeks ago.*

## O'HARA STRESS INDICATOR CHECKLIST
### PSYCHOLOGICAL RESPONSES TO STRESS

CIRCLE THE NUMBER WHICH BEST DESCRIBES the frequency of the occurrence of the following indicators of stress, and total your score.

|  | Seldom | Infrequent (not more than once a month) | Occasional (more than once per month) | Very Often (more than once per week) | Constant |
|---|---|---|---|---|---|
| Depression | 1 | 2 | 3 | 4 | 5 |
| Sense of hopelessness | 1 | 2 | 3 | 4 | 5 |
| Feeling of powerlessness | 1 | 2 | 3 | 4 | 5 |
| Low self-esteem | 1 | 2 | 3 | 4 | 5 |
| Frustration | 1 | 2 | 3 | 4 | 5 |
| Anger | 1 | 2 | 3 | 4 | 5 |
| Irritability | 1 | 2 | 3 | 4 | 5 |
| Resentment | 1 | 2 | 3 | 4 | 5 |
| Hostility | 1 | 2 | 3 | 4 | 5 |
| Anxiety in relationships | 1 | 2 | 3 | 4 | 5 |
| Anxiety over deadlines | 1 | 2 | 3 | 4 | 5 |
| Fearfulness | 1 | 2 | 3 | 4 | 5 |
| Boredom | 1 | 2 | 3 | 4 | 5 |
| Restlessness | 1 | 2 | 3 | 4 | 5 |

**TOTAL SCORE:**

**SCORE INTERPRETATION:**
**14-25** Comfortable handling stress ◆ **26-35** Could sharpen coping skills
**36-60** Time for changes ◆ **Over 60** Uncomfortable handling stress

# O'HARA STRESS SYMPTOMS CHECKLIST
## PHYSICAL RESPONSES TO STRESS

CIRCLE THE NUMBER WHICH BEST DESCRIBES the frequency of occurrence of the following symptoms, and then total your score.

| | Seldom | Infrequent (not more than once a month) | Occasional (more than once per month) | Very Often (more than once per week) | Constant |
|---|---|---|---|---|---|
| Migraine headache | 1 | 2 | 3 | 4 | 5 |
| Tension headache | 1 | 2 | 3 | 4 | 5 |
| Clammy hands/feet | 1 | 2 | 3 | 4 | 5 |
| Rapid shallow breath | 1 | 2 | 3 | 4 | 5 |
| Tightness in chest | 1 | 2 | 3 | 4 | 5 |
| Heart pounding | 1 | 2 | 3 | 4 | 5 |
| High blood pressure | 1 | 2 | 3 | 4 | 5 |
| Diarrhea | 1 | 2 | 3 | 4 | 5 |
| Constipation | 1 | 2 | 3 | 4 | 5 |
| Burping | 1 | 2 | 3 | 4 | 5 |
| Gassiness | 1 | 2 | 3 | 4 | 5 |
| Colitis | 1 | 2 | 3 | 4 | 5 |
| Increased urge to urinate | 1 | 2 | 3 | 4 | 5 |
| Indigestion | 1 | 2 | 3 | 4 | 5 |
| Backache | 1 | 2 | 3 | 4 | 5 |
| Neck pain | 1 | 2 | 3 | 4 | 5 |
| Dry mouth | 1 | 2 | 3 | 4 | 5 |
| Muscular tension | 1 | 2 | 3 | 4 | 5 |
| Sleeping difficulties | 1 | 2 | 3 | 4 | 5 |
| Fatigue | 1 | 2 | 3 | 4 | 5 |
| Dizziness | 1 | 2 | 3 | 4 | 5 |
| Menstrual distress | 1 | 2 | 3 | 4 | 5 |
| Ulcers | 1 | 2 | 3 | 4 | 5 |
| Tics/tremors | 1 | 2 | 3 | 4 | 5 |
| Jaw pain/tension | 1 | 2 | 3 | 4 | 5 |
| Skin rash | 1 | 2 | 3 | 4 | 5 |
| Asthma | 1 | 2 | 3 | 4 | 5 |
| Allergy | 1 | 2 | 3 | 4 | 5 |
| Gum chewing | 1 | 2 | 3 | 4 | 5 |
| Teeth grinding | 1 | 2 | 3 | 4 | 5 |
| Procrastinating | 1 | 2 | 3 | 4 | 5 |
| Irregular eating habits | 1 | 2 | 3 | 4 | 5 |
| Clenching fists | 1 | 2 | 3 | 4 | 5 |
| Nail biting | 1 | 2 | 3 | 4 | 5 |
| Rapid/loud talking | 1 | 2 | 3 | 4 | 5 |
| Emotional overreaction | 1 | 2 | 3 | 4 | 5 |
| Failure to complete projects | 1 | 2 | 3 | 4 | 5 |
| Doing several things simultaneously | 1 | 2 | 3 | 4 | 5 |

**TOTAL SCORE:**

**SCORE INTERPRETATION:**

**38-60** Comfortable handling stress ◆ **61-80** Could sharpen coping skills

**81-125** Time for changes ◆ **Over 125** Uncomfortable handling stress

# PART III

# PERSONALIZED STRESS MANAGEMENT

*The clouded sky of our minds may be brightened
by the sunlight of Peace and Joy.*

# LOWER BACK

# STRESS AND YOUR LOWER BACK

## The Problem

The magnitude of debilitating back problems in this country is staggering. Four out of every five Americans, regardless of age, sex, or occupation, will suffer acute back pain at some point in their lives. Back and neck pain are second only to the common cold as cause for sick leave. Over ten billion dollars is spent annually on research and patient care for back pain. A ruptured disc, scoliosis (curvature of the spine), congenital weaknesses, sciatica, tumors, muscular tension or spasming, poor posture, and overexertion are some of the possible causes of back pain. Emotional stress aggravates a potentially weak area through tensing of the muscles. The tensed muscles limit circulation, resulting in increased toxic build-up and reduced oxygen and nutrition to the cells in that area. Back surgery, performed to relieve excruciating pain usually associated with disc problems, has a discouraging success rate of less than 50%.

Encouraging news is that with proper rest, followed by gentle exercises, and then working into a sensible exercise routine, pain can be alleviated 90% of the time.

## The Solution

For personal back care, it is most important to get a professional diagnosis. A correct remedy is based on knowing exactly what the problem is. A herniated disc is treated differently from a strained ligament or a structural dysfunction.

The following exercises are specifically designed for those with chronic lumbar strain or trauma, not for those with other diagnosed pathologies. These exercises were developed by direct experience in healing a personal, severe chronic back strain of five years, and over eighteen years of working with physical therapists and physicians to develop exercises for relieving back pain for students and clients. Many, many people with differing causes for lower back pain have been greatly helped by this routine.

The solution is in maintaining a correct balance between flexibility and strength in the muscles, ligaments, and tendons that are involved in maintaining proper alignment of the lumbar spine. Overstretched or tight muscles affect the tilt of the pelvis and cause over- or under-arching of the lower back. These muscle groups include the abdominals, the iliopsoas (hip flexors), the hamstrings (backs of the thighs), the buttocks, and the external hip rotators. The vast majority of back discomfort is related to poor posture based on unequal balance of strength or flexibility in these muscles, or chronic, careless use of the spine due to incorrect lifting, soft mattresses, improper shoes, and overexertion. An acute back injury most often has a history based on the above lack of preventative back care.

The exercises presented here emphasize bringing these diverse muscle groups into balance so that the lumbar spine maintains correct alignment based on proper tilt of the pelvis. Almost 90% of Americans tend to overarch in the lumbar spine or, conversely, slouch at the lower back. Either position puts the spine out of alignment, and over time leads to chronic tension and pain.

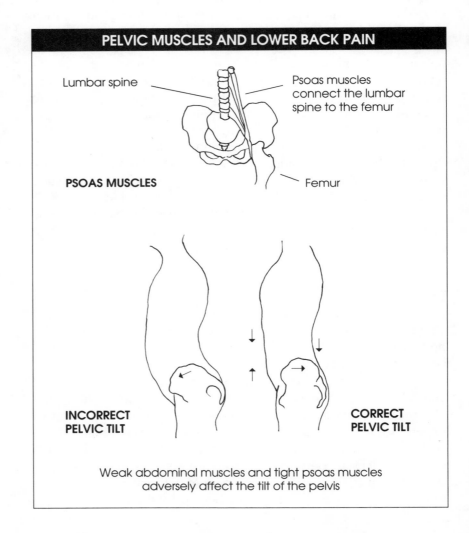

## PELVIC MUSCLES AND LOWER BACK PAIN

Lumbar spine

Psoas muscles connect the lumbar spine to the femur

**PSOAS MUSCLES**

Femur

**INCORRECT PELVIC TILT**

**CORRECT PELVIC TILT**

Weak abdominal muscles and tight psoas muscles adversely affect the tilt of the pelvis

Two especially important muscle groups to keep in balance to prevent overarching are the psoas and the abdominal muscles. The psoas is a major hip flexor connecting the femur (thigh bone) to the lumbar spine. Tight psoas muscles tip the pelvis forward and down, causing the back to overarch. This is accentuated if the abdominal muscles, which run parallel along the front of the spine between the base of the spine and the sternum, are weak. If you have tight psoas muscles and weak abdominal muscles, use the *Pelvic Tilt, Abdominal Strengthener,* and *Hip Flexor Stretch.* These exercises will strengthen the abdominals and stretch the psoas to correct the tilt of the pelvis.

The *Hamstring Stretch* and other exercises work on the muscle groups which are attached to the lumbar spine, and affect the tilt of the pelvis and help unlock the spine.

# CORRECT POSTURE

TO MAINTAIN A HEALTHY BACK and aid in the healing process, correct posture is essential. Posture plays a paramount role in the mechanical causes of pain. Whether sitting, lying down, or standing, to alleviate pain, consciously maintain correct alignment of the spine through good posture. Long hours at a desk, commuting, and relaxing in front of the television can aggravate the lumbar spine, especially if the spine is carelessly swayed forward or slouched back.

**TO ALLEVIATE PAIN**
Whether sitting, lying down, or standing, consciously maintain correct alignment of the spine through good posture.

Most chiropractic schools and physicians agree that correct standing posture is a straight line from the middle of the ear through the shoulder, hip, knee, and ankle. There is a slight natural curve at the neck and waist. Feel what correct posture is by standing with your back against the wall, with the buttocks, back of the chest, and back of the head touching the wall. There should be gaps between you and the wall only at the back of your neck and waist. Too much of a gap at the waist means the pelvis is tipped forward: The abdominal muscles may need strengthening, and the hamstrings and psoas may need stretching. If the waist is against the wall, the boat exercise will help regain the natural curve of the lumbar spine.

## To maintain a healthy lower back you need correct posture while:

### Sitting
Whether sitting, lying down, or standing, maintain the natural curves of your spine. The most common error in sitting is to slouch back at the waist. If you feel increased pain after sitting, perhaps you need a pillow at your lumbar spine for your chair or a change in chairs. The kneeler chairs have been successful for many people who sit for long periods of time. A rocking chair is also beneficial. Soft,

seemingly comfortable chairs lead to slouching and usually result in back pain. It is beneficial to sit in a chair with a firm back, with your knees higher than your hips. This position takes some pressure off the spine. When driving, bring your seat as close to the steering wheel as possible, keeping the knees higher than the hips. Use a little pillow in the lumbar area to maintain correct posture.

### Sleeping

If you wake up with a backache, it is highly likely you need a firmer mattress and/or a change in the way you sleep. A ¾-inch-thick piece of plywood under the entire mattress gives needed support to your spine. Also observe how you lie on the mattress. Lying on your stomach with your legs straight aggravates the lower back. Bend one knee and roll further onto your opposite side to lessen the arch of the spine. Sleeping on your back with a pillow under your thighs helps relieve pain. If you sleep on your side, place a pillow between your legs and keep them bent.

If you do not find it comfortable to sleep on your side with a pillow, experiment with bending one knee more than the other. I found it best to have the lower knee bent more than the upper knee, but the opposite may work in your situation. The idea is to stretch out the painful side; thus, it depends on which side you sleep on and which side of your spine has tense muscles. For example, if you sleep on your left side and your right side hurts, have your left leg bent more. If your left side hurts, bend the right leg more. Rather than figuring it out, *feel* which works better.

### Standing

While standing, constantly observe your posture and make any needed changes. Rest one foot on a little stool or several large books whenever standing for a length of time. For example, place one foot on a stack of books while doing the dishes. Alternate feet.

Obviously, using a stool or other prop is not possible at all times, but in casual situations do not hesitate to do it. Improvise! Experiment with how it feels to have one foot on a stool while standing; you will be surprised by the effects. A rapid source of relief is to place one foot at hip height, resting on a chair seat. Hold the position for several breaths and then repeat with the other leg.

**OBSERVE YOUR POSTURE**
While standing, constantly observe your posture and make any needed changes.

### Lifting heavy objects

Remember correct posture when moving heavy objects. While lifting an object, protect your back by using your legs, not your back. This means bending your knees and keeping your spine straight, rather than locking your knees and curling your back over the object. Carry the weight close to your body to prevent back strain.

# REGULAR EXERCISE

PRACTICE THE EXERCISES in this chapter every day, twice a day if possible. Couple the exercises with a routine of daily walking, swimming, or biking. These three sports are recommended by physical therapists and physicians for lower back syndrome. They keep the joints and spine supple, increase circulation, build muscle tone, and relieve tension. The choice of sport is left to you. Experiment with all three to discover both maximum benefit and enjoyment.

**WALKING, SWIMMING, OR BIKING**
These three sports are recommended by physical therapists and physicians for lower back syndrome.

## Swimming

If you swim, begin with the backstroke and then practice the side stroke (on both sides). As you get stronger, investigate the crawl (freestyle). Whereas practicing the crawl in a pool does not work well for me, doing the same stroke in the more buoyant ocean water is wonderful.

## Walking

If you choose to walk, gradually work up to several miles a day. There are many excellent walking shoes on the market. Walk to work, or part way if it is feasible. Use the stairs rather than the elevator. Take a walk after dinner or while waiting for a dinner reservation.

When my back was at its worst, I took long walks and found that going uphill felt the best. The upward slope requires you to tilt your pelvis and slightly tighten your abdominal muscles, which causes a relaxation reflex in the lower back. Hiking, excellent for stress management and lower back problems, could be the answer for you. The Sierra Club, *Prevention Magazine's* Walking Club, or a local walking association may be the support you need to get started.

## Biking

For some, biking is the answer. I did not find it helpful, but stories abound of its beneficial effects on relaxing the back, increasing vitality, reducing weight, and alleviating stress.

## Stretching

Any time you feel tension building, do something about it right away. For example, if you have been sitting for a while and want a quick release for the back, stand up and do *The Rope Climb* (page 70) and *Marching in Place* (page 47). If you have the time, walk briskly while doing a brief errand. You will be pleased by the effects of this stretch-and-walk break.

To a large extent, once you have been diagnosed, it is up to you to be your own best doctor. Follow the routines in this chapter, or one recommended by your doctor, and take responsibility for making changes that best suit your particular situation. If a position increases discomfort, stop what you are doing immediately.

Practiced regularly and personalized to your situation, the exercises in this chapter could be your solution to a healthy back. Choosing one of the three sports to go with the exercises will aid in the healing process. They also allow you the time to reduce stress. Practice the breathing and mental exercises given in earlier chapters in conjunction with your chosen activity. *Good luck!*

## STAGE ONE: ONSET OF PAIN

BEGIN BY RELIEVING PAIN through rest and your doctor's advice and possible prescription. Next, start the exercises listed in Stage One. Although these exercises are progressive in their order, and are designed for relieving back pain, each person has his own rhythm of recovery. As you begin the exercises, listen to your body and respond accordingly—if one exercise isn't helpful, move on to another one.

See the At-A-Glance review of the exercises at the end of the chapter. First, read the detailed instructions.

### Stage One Exercises
Rest
Alternate Knees to Chest
Lumbar Massage
Pelvic Tilt

# DETAILED INSTRUCTIONS ON STAGE ONE EXERCISES

## Rest

If pain is due to an injury, the best generally accepted prescription is rest, ice, compression, and elevation of the injured area for 24-48 hours. Always seek the medical advice of trained emergency technicians or a physician. If pain has developed gradually, again consult with a physician.

Time is the best healer. Except in the rare situation when emergency surgery is required, physicians recommend an initial stage of rest and perhaps a muscle relaxant. How long you should rest is now under question. For lower back pain not caused by nerve injury, the usual treatment has been a minimum of seven days of bed rest. However, a 1986 study of 203 patients at the Seattle Veterans' Administration Medical Center indicated that only two days of bed rest was better. After three months, those who initially rested in bed for only two days had missed 45% fewer days of work than the longer-resting group. Follow your physician's advice.

How you rest is important. It is usually most comfortable and beneficial to lie on your back on a firm mattress with a large pillow under your thighs. This gently decompresses the lumbar spine. Experiment with the size of pillow. You may find it most comfortable to lie on the carpet with your calves resting on the seat of a chair.

Other means of temporary relief are relaxing in a jacuzzi or warm bath, or having a gentle massage by a massage therapist.

Once the pain subsides, specific gentle exercises help release the muscular tension. After consultation with your doctor, practice the following exercises each morning and evening. Stop the practice if there is any discomfort.

## Alternate Knees to Chest

Lie on your back, with the soles of your feet next to your buttocks. Bend one knee into the chest, clasping your hands around the shin. Alternate legs, holding the knee to the chest for one complete breath. Consciously relax the lower back as you exhale. Practice five times on each side.

Alternate Knees to Chest

Lumbar Massage (First Position)

Lumbar Massage (Second Position)

## Lumbar Massage

**First Position:** Bend your knees to your chest with your hands clasped around your thighs and rock sideways for a minute.

**Second Position:** Remain in the first position. Now cross your feet at your ankles, take hold of your feet, and continue rocking for another minute. Concentrate on relaxing in the area being massaged.

Pelvic Tilt

## Pelvic Tilt

Lie on your back with your feet parallel, near your buttocks. Gently stretch the lumbar spine by contracting your abdominal muscles and pushing the small of your back towards the carpet. Keep your buttocks muscles relaxed. Hold the contracted position for two breaths. Relax the back to its natural curve. Repeat two more times.

To increase the stretch of the lumbar spine, tighten the buttocks and lift them two to three inches off the carpet. Hold the contracted position for two breaths. Relax back down to the carpet. Repeat the exercise two more times.

## STAGE TWO: RELIEVING CHRONIC LOW BACK PAIN

Continue the process of recovery by adding the following exercises to your practice. For those with a history of chronic pain or intermittent tension, follow the same routine, including the above-listed exercises. Follow your physician's recommendations.

### Stage Two Exercises

Resting Lumbar Stretch

Lower Back Release

Inner Thigh Stretch

Twist on Your Back

Hamstring Stretch

Abdominal Strengthener

Spinal Twist on Back, Legs Crossed

Hip Flexor Stretch

The Boat

The Fallen Leaf

Anti-Gravity Exercises

## DETAILED INSTRUCTIONS ON STAGE TWO EXERCISES

### Resting Lumbar Stretch

**First Position:** Sit sideways next to the wall and then lean back and swing your legs up the wall, with your knees bent at a comfortable angle. Have your buttocks approximately a foot from the wall. Rest your legs against the back of a chair if wall space is not handy. Place your arms over your head on the floor with your palms toward the ceiling. As you inhale, stretch the back of your neck and your lower back by pushing them toward the floor (straightening and stretching the spine), and flex your heels toward the ceiling. As you exhale, relax your arms, spine, and legs while remaining in the same position. Repeat for three more breaths.

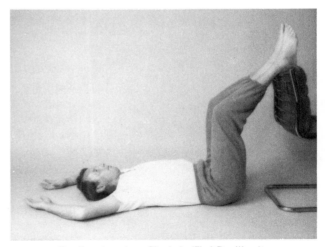

Resting Lumbar Stretch (First Position)

Resting Lumbar Stretch
(Second Position)

**Second Position:** Remain on your back, and bring your hands to your sides. Begin by inhaling. Completely fill your lungs by relaxing your abdominal muscles, then expanding your rib cage, and lastly filling your upper chest. You will feel a slight contraction in your neck when you have reached your full lung capacity. As you exhale, relax your neck muscles, contract at the ribs, and squeeze your abdominal muscles. Take five *Complete Breaths.*

## Lower Back Release

This exercise relieves lower back pain if it is related to tense or tight buttocks and outer thigh muscles. Remain with your legs up the wall or resting on the back of a chair.

**First Position:** While still lying on your back with your legs up the wall, bend your left knee into your chest, and then turn the knee out to the side and rest your ankle beside the right thigh or on it, just above the right knee.

Lower Back Release (First Position)

(Second Position)

**Second Position:** Stretch the left buttock muscles by gently pressing the left knee towards the wall or, if your ankle is resting on the thigh, slowly slide the right foot a few inches, so that the sole of the right foot is against the wall and you feel a stretch in the left buttock and thigh. Leave your buttocks on the carpet. Take six *Diaphragmatic Breaths* in this position. Relax your abdominal muscles as you inhale, and contract them as your exhale.

## Inner Thigh Stretch

You can increase mobility in the external hip rotators with this exercise. Bend your knees to your chest, placing the soles of your feet against the wall close to your buttocks, then open the knees out to the sides. If a wall is not accessible, use the back of a chair or hold your ankles. Place your hands just above the knees and gently press the legs open. If this is uncomfortable, practice by holding your ankles with your hands and pressing the knees open with your elbows. Take three *Diaphragmatic Breaths* in this position. Bring the knees together.

Inner Thigh Stretch

## Twist on Your Back

This exercise stretches out the rotators of the lumbar spine.

**First Position:** Keep your knees bent to your chest, in the position in which you completed the *Inner Thigh Stretch*.

**Second Position:** Bring your arms out to shoulder height on the floor. Lower both legs to the left and turn your head to the right. Place a pillow or two under your legs to lessen the stretch. Take three *Complete Breaths* in this position. As you inhale, completely fill the chest and focus on the upper body stretch. As you exhale, relax from your waist down to your toes. Let each exhalation help you relax more deeply. Repeat to the right side.

Twist on Your Back (First Position)

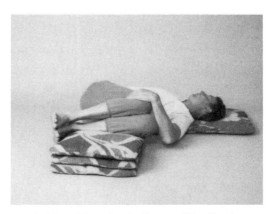
Twist on Your Back (Second Position)

## Hamstring Stretch

Tight hamstrings can aggravate lower back problems by affecting the tilt of the pelvis.

**First Position:** Come away from the wall or chair and lie on your back with your feet on the floor close to your buttocks. Place a belt, towel, or strap around the sole of your right foot and start straightening your knee. Keep the knee bent several inches: The tighter your hamstrings, the more bent you should keep your knee. Have your elbows straight, as far up the strap as possible. If you feel any strain in your neck, place a pillow under your head or gently tuck your chin towards your chest.

**Second Position:** Keeping the buttocks on the floor and concentrating on the back of the right thigh, gently pull on the strap by bending your

Hamstring Stretch (First Position)

Hamstring Stretch (Second Position)

elbows, bringing the "straight" leg closer to your face. Bend your right knee more if the stretch is behind the knee rather than in the back of the thigh. Take six *Diaphragmatic Breaths* in this position, focusing on relaxing the hamstrings at the back of the thigh with each exhalation.

## Abdominal Strengthener

**First Position:** Practice abdominal curls with your calves resting on the seat of a chair, or the soles of your feet on the carpet by your buttocks with your knees bent. In both positions be sure to do the work with your abdominal muscles, not your neck. As you exhale, tighten your abdominals, tuck your chin to your chest, and roll your head, shoulders, and upper torso towards your knees. As you inhale, slowly lower back down to the carpet and relax your abdominal muscles. Begin with five repetitions and work up to fifteen.

Abdominal Strengthener (First Position)

Abdominal Strengthener (Second Position)

**Second Position:** To strengthen the obliques (the muscles that extend to your sides from the abdominal muscles), bring your head and torso alternately to each knee so that there is a slight twist. Bring your head towards each knee five times. Over a period of a month, bring the number of repetitions up to fifteen.

## Spinal Twist on Back, Legs Crossed

Replace the *Spinal Twist on Back, Legs Parallel* with this exercise when you feel the need for a greater stretch than the parallel leg position allows.

**First Position:** Stretch out on your back bending your knees to your chest. Clasp your hands around your legs and gently stretch your lower back. Cross the left leg over the right leg at the thighs and stretch your arms out at shoulder height, with your palms against the carpet. Inhale, keeping the legs close to your chest.

**Second Position:** As you exhale, lower your legs to the right side of your body and turn your head to the left. Take six *Diaphragmatic Breaths* in this position, relaxing your lower back, legs, and feet with each exhalation. Keep the knees as close to your chest as you can. It is more important to keep both shoulders on the carpet than to get the legs to the carpet. Press your right elbow into the carpet to help keep the left shoulder down. If your lower back is still a bit tight and your feet and legs do not touch the carpet, place a pillow by your right side and lower the legs to the pillow rather than the carpet. The key is to relax more deeply with each exhalation. Concentrate on your legs and lower back. By the end of six breaths you will have relaxed at least six inches deeper into the stretch, giving a wonderful release to your lower back. Bring the legs back to the first position.

**Third Position:** Leaving the legs crossed, lower them to your left and take six more *Diaphragmatic Breaths*. Again, use a pillow if needed. Be sure to keep the thighs close to your chest to prevent the lumbar spine from arching. Use your hand to pull the legs closer to your chest. Bring the legs back to the first position.

Repeat the exercise with your right leg crossed over your left leg.

Spinal Twist on Back, Legs Crossed (First Position)

Spinal Twist on Back, Legs Crossed (Second Position)

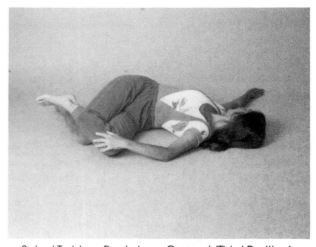
Spinal Twist on Back, Legs Crossed (Third Position)

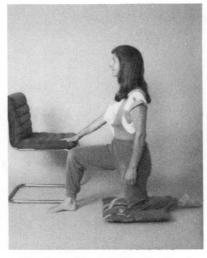
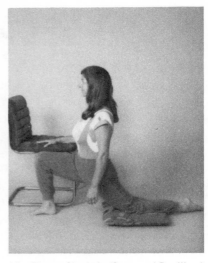

Hip Flexor Stretch (First Position)      Hip Flexor Stretch (Second Position)

## Hip Flexor Stretch

**First Position:** To stretch out the iliopsoas muscles in the hip flexor, kneel on a blanket next to the wall or a chair. Holding onto the chair for support, bring one foot out in front of you, with the thigh parallel to the floor. Lift through your chest and gently flatten the back into a pelvic tilt by tightening the abdominals and tensing the buttocks muscles.

**Second Position:** Keeping the pelvic tilt, slowly increase the bend of the front knee until you feel a stretching in the groin area of the other leg. Hold for three breaths and then repeat with the other leg. Keep the pelvis tucked throughout the exercise.

Some people find kneeling on the floor difficult. If so, get the same stretch by standing, facing a chair, and placing one foot on the seat of

The Boat (First Position)

The Boat (Second Position)      The Boat (Third Position)

the chair with a bent knee. Keeping the pelvis tilted by tightening the abdominal muscles, shortening the distance between the pubic bone and the breast bone, increase the bend of the knee. Practice on both sides.

## The Boat

*The Boat* is an excellent exercise for strengthening the paraspinal muscles and buttocks muscles, but do *not* practice it if your lower back is in pain.

Begin with the first and second positions. As you feel stronger, add the third position.

**First Position:** Begin by lying down on your stomach with your arms at your sides and your legs together. Lift the head, chest, arms, and legs off the ground and hold for three breaths. An indication of weak lumbar muscles is the inability to get the thighs off the floor. In your initial practice, before doing the second position, release the lower back by doing *The Fallen Leaf,* as described below in the next exercise.

**Second Position:** Remain on your stomach and place your arms out on the floor at shoulder height and your legs approximately two feet apart. As in the first position, lift your head, legs, and arms off the floor. Hold for three breaths.

**Third Position:** A more difficult variation of the first position is to start with the legs together and the arms over your head on the floor. Lift as in the previous variations. Hold for three breaths.

In all three positions, lengthen through the back of the neck by pulling the shoulders back and down. Do not arch the neck back. Let the neck be an extension of correct spinal alignment. Do not tilt the chin up.

## The Fallen Leaf

**First Position:** Do not end *The Boat* by remaining on your stomach. After you have practiced one or more of the variations, complete the exercise by placing your hands under your shoulders, bending your knees, and coming up onto your hands and knees, with your back curled towards the ceiling.

**Second Position:** From the first position, lower your buttocks to your heels. Hold for three breaths, breathing slowly, relaxing your lower back as you exhale.

The Fallen Leaf (First Position)

The Fallen Leaf (Second Position)

The Squat (First Position)

The Squat (Second Position)

## The Squat

**First Position:** Open a door and, hanging onto both door knobs, squat down, letting your heels come off the floor. Once in the squatting position, slowly lower your heels to stretch the lumbar spine. Initially, practice with your feet apart and toes turned out. Lower your heels onto a book to lessen the stretch. Gradually work towards practicing with the feet parallel and heels on the floor. Hold for three breaths.

     **Second Position (advanced):** Squat down, remaining on your toes, and rest your elbows and forearms on your thighs. Press into your thighs with your arms and lengthen the torso out of the hips to release the back. As your back and legs get stronger and more supple, keep your heels down. Let your hands rest on the ground in front of you or press your palms together. Keep the knees over your toes by pressing the elbows into the thighs. Hold the position for six breaths, concentrating on relaxing the lower back.

# ANTI-GRAVITY EXERCISES

THERE ARE NUMEROUS ANTI-GRAVITY devices for giving a quick release to the lower back. They vary from back swings to boots that hook to a horizontal pole so that you hang from your heels.

## Hanging

Install a bar across a doorway several inches from the top. Whenever you need a quick release, take hold of the bar and hang. These bars are not hard to buy, as people use them for chin-ups and other exercises.

     Another form of hanging, which sometimes stretches out unequal muscle tension enough to allow the spine to correct its alignment, is to place your hands on the kitchen sink, a car fender, or a sturdy table and straighten your arms to lift your body off the ground with your pelvis against the sink, fender, or table.

## AT-A-GLANCE AN ILLUSTRATED REVIEW OF LOWER BACK EXERCISES

**STAGE ONE EXERCISES**

1) Rest

2) Alternate Knees to Chest

3) Lumbar Massage (First Position)

3) Lumbar Massage (Second Position)

4) Pelvic Tilt

## AT-A-GLANCE AN ILLUSTRATED REVIEW OF LOWER BACK EXERCISES

**STAGE TWO EXERCISES**

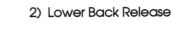

1) Resting Lumbar Stretch (In Two Positions)

2) Lower Back Release

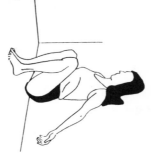

3) Inner Thigh Stretch

4) Lower Back Twist (In Two Positions)

5) Hamstring Stretch (In Two Positions)

6) Abdominal Strenghtener (In Two Positions)

7) Spinal Twist on Back, Legs Crossed (In Three Positions)

8) Hip Flexor Stretch (In Two Positions)

9) The Boat
(In Three Positions)

10) The Fallen Leaf (In Two Positions)

11) The Squat

12) Rest

ADVANCED

# ADVANCED STRETCHING AND STRENGTHENING EXERCISES

IF YOU HAVE BEEN PRACTICING the exercises in the last five weeks or are an athlete who is flexible and needs a warm-up or cool down program, the following routine is suitable for you. The exercises incorporate stretching and strengthening and are excellent as an advanced stress management system. They are based on yoga postures and are recognized for their numerous health benefits, including flexibility conditioning, improving circulation, muscular toning, and reducing physical and mental stress.

Do the exercises as taught in the earlier chapters: with attention on the breathing, and holding the positions for three or six breaths. The longer period allows for a deeper stretching or strengthening of the muscles. Do what feels best for you. Challenge yourself, but do not strain. The routine takes approximately twenty minutes to complete. The exercises are in a specific order to maximize benefits and safety.

## Advanced Exercises Routine

Warm-ups

The Sun Salutation

The Triangle

Half Spinal Twist

Simple Inverted Pose

Spinal Twist On Back

The Bow

The Fallen Leaf

USE THE AT-A-GLANCE SECTION at the end of the chapter after you understand how to do the exercises correctly.

# DETAILED INSTRUCTIONS ON THE ADVANCED EXERCISES

## Warm-ups

FOR THE NECK, SHOULDERS, HIPS, SPINE, AND HAMSTRINGS
Begin in the standing position with your eyes closed and take three *Complete Breaths*.

The following warm-ups are in the At-A-Glance illustrations at the end of this chapter. Detailed descriptions are in previous chapters, as listed.

Practice the *Neck and Shoulder Arch and Curl* as taught in *Week Two* (page 47).

Next practice *The Rope Climb* as taught in *Week Three* (page 70).

Continue with the *Standing Spinal Twist* as taught in *Week Two* (page 48), but before coming out of the partial squat position, drop deeper into the squat and flatten your back. Place your hands on your ankles and gently push your elbows against your legs to increase the stretch of the inner thighs. Hold for three breaths. Come up slowly and shake out the legs.

Now go into *The Rag Doll* as taught in *Week One* (page 28). Before coming out of the position, stretch a bit deeper by straightening the legs and the spine, and hold for three more breaths. It feels good to bring both hands to the outside of one ankle and get a slight twist in the stretch. Practice to both sides. Come up slowly with a curled spine and knees bent two inches or more. Briefly keep the chin tucked while in the standing position to prevent dizziness.

## The Sun Salutation

This exercise stimulates circulation, strengthens and stretches the spine, stretches the hip flexors and hamstrings, and has an overall invigorating effect. It is different from the other exercises because it flows from one position to the next without stopping. There are twelve positions. Inhale or exhale during movement between positions. While extending deeper into a position, you can briefly pause in your breathing or take one *Complete Breath*. Once you have the rhythm, feel the fluidity of the movement, like the tides of the ocean coming in and going out.

**First Position:** Begin in the standing posture with your hands at your chest in prayer position.

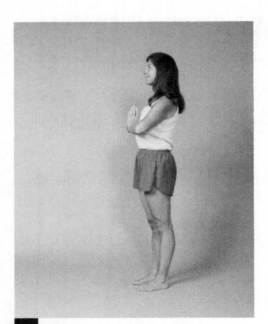

1 The Sun Salutation (First Position)

**2** The Sun Salutation (Second Position)

**3** The Sun Salutation (Third Position)

**Second Position:** In one continuous movement, inhale and stretch your arms out in from of you, palms together at shoulder height, and then over your head with arms parallel and the palms facing each other. Tighten your buttocks and lift through the chest and arch back, keeping your head between your arms. Hold the breath and the position only long enough to feel the full extension. If you feel any tension in the lower back, keep it an upper body stretch by focusing on lifting and arching through the chest.

**Third Position:** Exhale, and with a continuous fluid movement, bend forward from the hips. Extend your arms and spine first towards the wall and then towards the carpet. Place your hands next to your feet. Leave the breath out only long enough to fully stretch the hamstrings and spine. If you cannot reach the carpet, bend your knees to place your hands beside your feet.

**Fourth Position:** While inhaling, step back with the right foot, and lower the right knee to the carpet. The left knee should be directly over the left ankle. Pause long enough to extend into the right hip flexor. To further increase the stretch in the right hip flexor, press against the toes of your right foot and push your hips forward. Open through the chest and look forward.

**4** The Sun Salutation (Fourth Position)

**5** The Sun Salutation (Fifth Position)

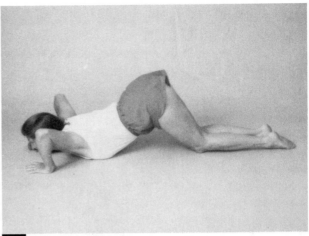

**6** The Sun Salutation (Sixth Position)

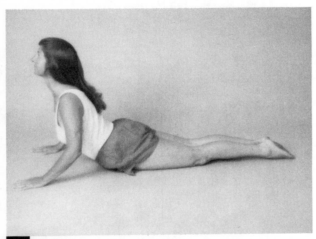

**7** The Sun Salutation (Seventh Position)

**Fifth Position:** Exhale while stepping back into a man's push-up position. Lengthen the body by pressing the heels towards one wall and the top of the head towards the other wall. Press evenly into your hands. Do not arch your back.

**Sixth Position:** Leave the breath out and drop your knees to the carpet. Begin inhaling, and lower your chest and chin to the carpet, leaving your buttocks high.

**Seventh Position:** Continue the inhalation and move the chest forward between your arms until you are stretched out on the carpet. Press into your hands and lift the upper torso off the carpet. The navel should remain on the carpet, the buttocks tight and the elbows bent and close to the body, hands under your shoulders. This position is called *The Cobra*. To increase the strengthening of your mid-back, begin with very little weight on your hands. Gradually press your palms into the carpet, keeping your elbows bent and shoulders pulled back and down. Do not hunch the shoulders; look straight ahead, lengthening the back of the neck. To bring a stretch into the lower back, gradually straighten the elbows and soften the buttocks muscles. If you have a weak lower back, do *The Boat* (page 150) rather than *The Cobra*.

**Eighth Position:** Exhale while curling your toes under and pushing your buttocks up towards the ceiling into the *Inverted V* position (page 123). If you have a weak lower back, bend your knees before pushing your buttocks up. If your hamstrings are tight, walk your feet in a few inches towards your hands. Hold the *Inverted V* position while inhaling and exhaling.

8  The Sun Salutation (Eighth Position)

9  The Sun Salutation (Ninth Position)

*While inhaling,* extend into your hands evenly and lengthen through the arms and spine, pushing the buttocks towards the ceiling. If your back curls because of tight hamstrings, bend the knees so you can straighten the spine. Gradually work to straighten the knees as you gain flexibility. *While exhaling,* relax your neck. Press your chest towards your thighs and your heels towards the carpet. Tighten the abdominal muscles to elongate the torso as you complete your exhalation.

**Ninth Position:** Inhale, bringing the right foot forward between the hands and lowering the left knee to the carpet. Look forward, and lift the chest. Keep the right knee over the right ankle to protect the knee.

**Tenth Position:** Exhale and step forward with the left foot, coming into a forward bend. Immediately straighten the spine and legs for correct alignment. Stretch the top of the head towards the carpet rather than towards the knees. If you have a weak lower back or tight hamstrings, keep the knees bent and the spine curled, as in *The Rag Doll.*

10  The Sun Salutation (Tenth Position)

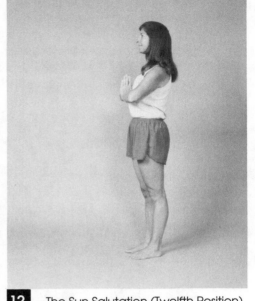

**11** The Sun Salutation (Eleventh Pos.)     **12** The Sun Salutation (Twelfth Position)

**Eleventh Position:** Inhale as you come up. If you have a weak lower back, come up with a curled spine and soft knees as in *The Rag Doll.* If your back is strong, come up with a flat back and straight knees, arms extended straight out. Continue the upward movement and arch back, buttocks tight and chest lifted.

**Twelfth Position:** Now exhale and return to the standing posture with the hands in a prayer position at the chest.

Repeat *The Sun Salutation* four to six times. Upon completion, close the eyes, take three *Complete Breaths,* and then observe the exhilarating effects of the exercise.

## The Triangle

**First Position:** Start in the standing posture and place your feet wider apart than your hips. Keeping your hips forward, pivot on your left heel ninety degrees. Push your right heel back counter-clockwise approximately thirty degrees. Inhale and bring your arms out to the side palms down.

Exhale, pulling your hips towards the right and your left arm to the left until your trunk is stretched sideways. From this position, lower your left hand onto your shin, your ankle, or the carpet. Stretch the right arm up towards the ceiling. Slightly tucking the chin to keep the back of the neck in alignment, turn and look at the upstretched hand. Take three *Diaphragmatic Breaths* in this position. As you inhale, concentrate on pulling the chest back into line with the knee and lengthening the torso. As you exhale, press against the lower hand to roll further open with your trunk. Although breathing diaphragmatically, keep the abdominals tight and the buttocks tucked to protect the lower back.

**Second Position:** To increase the stretch, bring the right arm over by your ear and look straight forward. Keep the triangle balanced by pushing into the outside of your back heel and using your right hip as an anchor point from which to stretch. Take three *Diaphragmatic Breaths* in this position. Do not hyperextend (lock) the left knee. Soften it if you feel a strain.

To come out of the position, bring the right arm up towards the ceiling, and then soften the left knee slightly and use your abdominal muscles to lift you up. Turn your left foot forward, lower your arms to the side, and step your feet together. Repeat the stretch to the other side.

One way to practice the triangle is to do it using a wall. Stand with your back to the wall and your feet two inches from the wall.

The Triangle (First Position)

The Triangle (Second Position)

Going into the full stretch, feel your torso and shoulders against the wall, chest open and pelvis tucked. Keep the lower back, the top hip, and the shoulders as much against the wall as you can. This encourages the correct position and intensifies the side stretch. Do not let the quadricep roll in. Protect the front knee by rolling the quadricep out so that the knee is not twisted. This is more important than going down to the floor with your palm.

## Half Spinal Twist

This posture works the rotators of the spine, giving the spine lateral flexibility. It stretches the inner hip muscles and aids digestion.

**First Position:** Begin by sitting on the edge of a pillow with your legs straight. Bend the right knee and pull the right foot under the left leg. Place it next to the left hip. Bend the left knee and place the left foot to the outside of the right knee. Twist towards the left knee with the upper body, bringing the right upper arm to the

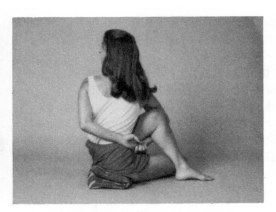

Half Spinal Twist (First Position)          Half Spinal Twist (Second Position)

outside of the left thigh. Grasp the right knee or the left foot with your right hand. Place the left hand close to your buttocks, pushing your weight forward and elongating the spine. Take three breaths in this position, concentrating on lifting up out of the hips and opening the chest on the inhalation, and relaxing the left hip and twisting further on the exhalation. Do not force the rotation.

**Second Position:** This position takes the stretch into the middle and upper back. Bend the right elbow and wrist and bring your hand under your left thigh. At the same time bring your left arm around your back at your waist. Clasp your left hand around your right hand or wrist. Take three breaths in this position. Relax out of the position. Repeat to the other side. For more of a stretch through the ribs and chest, take three *Three-Part Rhythmic Breaths* in this position.

Simple Inverted Pose (First Position)

## Simple Inverted Pose

This posture increases circulation in the upper lungs and brings oxygenated blood to the brain. It is excellent for tired legs and feet.

Do not practice this exercise if you have high blood pressure, a weak heart, diabetes, or diseases of the eyes or sinuses. Women should not practice this posture during their menstrual periods.

**First Position:** Stretch out on the carpet and take three *Complete Breaths* in the deep relaxation position. Bring your legs together and hands by your side. Inhale, and then as you exhale, tighten your abdominals, flatten your lower back into the carpet, and raise your legs towards the ceiling. Hold this position and inhale, flexing your heels and tucking your chin to stretch the back of your neck.

**Second Position:** Exhale, bend your knees, and push with your finger tips to help lift your buttocks off the carpet. Curl your spine and bring your knees towards or to your forehead. Place your hands on your back to help support your spine. Take three

*Diaphragmatic Breaths* in this position. There should be no straining. This part of the exercise is called *The Tranquility Pose*. If the position does not feel restful to you, practice earlier exercises to stretch the spine and hamstrings until you can do it with enjoyment.

If you can balance in this position without your hands on your spine, remove your hands, clasp your fingers together, and extend your arms straight out on the carpet. Roll your shoulders open and bring the elbows towards each other.

**Third Position:** Bend your elbows again and let your buttocks drop into the hands with the fingers near the *base* of the spine. Straighten the legs and lift them up to a forty-five-degree angle to the floor. Hold for three breaths.

(Second Position)

(Third Position)

(Fourth Position)

**Fourth Position:** If you are comfortable in the third position, keep lifting the legs until they are perpendicular to the floor. Straighten the spine by lifting the chest towards the ceiling and stretching both sides of the ribs equally. Hold for six breaths. Keep the hands at the base of the spine to keep pressure off the neck.

To come out of the position, bend the knees towards the forehead, place your arms by your sides on the carpet, and lower your spine and legs to the carpet.

## Spinal Twist

Practice one of the spinal twists on your back: with the legs crossed (pages 30 and 149), or the legs parallel (page 51), or with one leg bent (page 72).

The Bow

## The Bow

This posture stretches and strengthens the spine, increases flexibility in the shoulders and hip flexors, and strengthens the quadriceps. Do not do this posture if you have a ruptured disc, high blood pressure, or pain in your lower back.

Lie down on your stomach with your legs apart, and bend your knees. Reach back and take hold of your ankles. Lift your head, chest, and thighs off the carpet, pushing your feet into your hands to help lift the thighs. Lift as high as you can. Next bring your knees parallel, hip distance apart. Pull down through your shoulders and squeeze your shoulder blades together. Keep the buttocks tight. Hold for three to six breaths and continue to lift the thighs as high as you can. Release the legs and lower onto your stomach.

## Fallen Leaf

*The Fallen Leaf* (page 151) releases tension in the lower back and gently stretches the spine. From *The Bow,* come into *The Cat* by placing your hands under your shoulders and then straightening your arms and bending your knees. Curl your spine towards the ceiling. Keeping the curl, *slowly* lower your buttocks to your heels. Hold for three breaths, stretching through your arms and flattening your back. For more of a stretch, separate your legs and bring your chest to the carpet.

For an additional hip stretch, bring your knees together, place your hands wide of your knees and bring your right hip to the carpet, keeping your chest on your thighs. Take three breaths in this position. Repeat with the other hip.

Return to *The Fallen Leaf* position and then raise your trunk so you are sitting upright. Sit quietly with your eyes closed, breathing slowly and deeply.

## Deep Relaxation

Conclude with a deep relaxation, consciously relaxing mentally and physically.

## Summary of the Benefits of the Advanced Routine

Upon completion of this routine you will feel refreshed and relaxed. The warm-ups and the advanced stretching and strengthening exercises release your physically stored emotional tension. Your attention to relaxing more deeply through the breathing will increase the calming effects of the routine. *The Sun Salutation* and *The Bow* will stretch out your tense muscles and delightfully invigorate you.

# AT-A-GLANCE AN ILLUSTRATED REVIEW OF ADVANCED EXERCISES

## WARM-UPS

1) Neck and Shoulder Arch and Curl (In Three Positions)

2) The Rope Climb

3) Standing Spinal Twist

4) The Rag Doll

## THE SUN SALUTATION

6) The Triangle (In Two Positions)

7) Half Spinal Twist (In Two Positions)

8) Simple Inverted Pose (In Four Positions)

9) The Bow

10) The Fallen Leaf (In Two Positions)

11) Deep Relaxation

**NINE TO FIVE**

# STRETCHING NINE TO FIVE

SITTING FOR LONG HOURS AT A DESK, even with attention to correct posture, leads to a buildup of muscular tension, poor circulation, and lack of mental clarity. Research has conclusively shown the benefit of relaxation, stretching, and breathing exercises for reduction of tension, pain, and stress.

When you are physically and mentally relaxed, your productivity rises and you feel better. Stretching, combined with conscious deep breathing, prevents an accumulation of tension and resulting pain. To prevent muscular tension, nervous fatigue, and anxiety, enjoy these three-minute routines throughout your day.

EVERY THIRTY MINUTES perform a few stretches. To activate different muscle groups, vary which exercises you practice. For example:

1. For your first break do several *Neck and Shoulder Arch and Curls* (page 47), *The Rope Climb* (page 70), and the *Shoulder and Chest Stretch* (page 70).

2. Twenty minutes later practice the *Palm Press* (page 28), and *The Palm Press and Sway* (page 124), and *The Cat* (page 28), curling and arching the spine while sitting in your chair. End with *Straight Arm Rotations* (page 71).

3. For a third routine, practice the *Standing Spinal Twist* (page 48), the *Standing Side Stretch* (page 48), and the *Full Body Stretch* using your chair (page 31).

4. For a fourth routine, take three *Complete Breaths*, inhaling, tensing the whole body, and exhaling, relaxing the body from head to toe. With your eyes closed, sit for two minutes, breathing naturally. As you inhale, visualize ocean waves breaking at the shore. Let the waves wash through you, dissolving tension and anxiety. As you exhale, let the waves cleanse the mind, removing your worries with your exhalation.

IF STOPPING EVERY THIRTY MINUTES is too time-consuming for you, practice the stretches, breathing exercises, and relaxation on your breaks. Stretch and breathe when you go to the rest room, on your coffee breaks, during lunch, and just as you leave the office. You will quickly recognize the benefits of practicing these short routines throughout the day. Do not be surprised to find others asking to join you. Many students have told me that this has turned into a pleasant connection with fellow employees and employers. Have fun with it and take turns leading and creating stretches. All the neck and shoulder exercises, many of the standing exercises, and the ones presented below will give you a good release from physical and mental stress. The following routines were favorite ones I worked out while writing this book. They provided excellent relief during hours at the computer. I hope you find them as enjoyable and relaxing as I have!

## Office Routine One

Shoulder Stretch

Shoulder Shrugs

Wrist and Finger Stretch

Spinal Relaxer

Nose-towards-Knee Stretch

Spinal Twist

Lower Back Release

Shoulder Stretch

Shoulder Shrugs

Wrist and Finger Stretch

# DETAILED INSTRUCTIONS ON OFFICE ROUTINE ONE

### Shoulder Stretch
To release upper-middle back tension, hold left arm just below the elbow with your right hand and pull your elbow toward your right shoulder. Hold for three breaths. Repeat to the other side.

### Shoulder Shrugs
To relax tension in the shoulders and neck, rotate your shoulders in large circles. Push your shoulder blades together, lift the shoulders as high toward the ears as possible, curl them forward, and then pull them down towards the floor. Rotate slowly three times in each direction, using your full range of motion.

Spinal Relaxer

### Wrist and Finger Stretch
Stretch your arm out in front of you with the palm facing away, using the other hand to bend the fingers back towards you. Repeat with the other hand. Shake both hands from the wrists sideways and back and forth to relieve tension.

### Spinal Relaxer
To relax the spine, lower back, and shoulders, and to help increase blood flow to the brain, place your feet parallel on the carpet and curl forward in your chair, relaxing your neck, shoulders, and back. Allow the chest to relax on the thighs and the hands to relax toward the carpet. Hold for three complete breaths. Come up with a curled spine.

Nose-toward-Knee Stretch

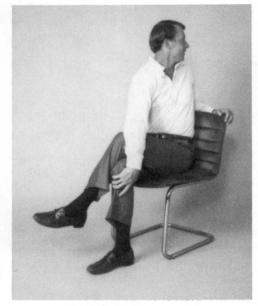

Spinal Twist

Lower Back Release

### Nose-toward-Knee Stretch
To stretch the back of the thighs and to release neck and shoulder tension, pull one leg to your chest and lower your head toward the knee. Lift the shoulders high, by your ears, as you hold the knee with both hands. Hold for three breaths.

### Spinal Twist
To release tension in the lower back, sit away from the back of your chair and cross your legs at your thighs. Place your hand along the top outside of the opposite thigh and the other hand on the back of your chair. Look over your back shoulder. Sit with good posture, lifting your chest, lengthening your spine, and pulling your shoulders down. Take three *Three-Part Rhythmic Breaths*. Turn forward, and repeat to the other side.

### Lower Back Release
To stretch the buttocks muscles and relieve lower back tension, sit on the edge of a chair with both feet on the floor. Lift your left leg and place your left ankle onto your right thigh. Place your left hand on your left thigh and press. To increase the stretch, bend forward from your hips and place your forearms on your left lower leg (as in the photo). Take three slow breaths, consciously relaxing your buttocks muscles as you exhale. Repeat on the other side.

Neck Rolls

### Office Routine Two
Neck Rolls
Chest Expander
Upper Back and Shoulder Release
Elbow-to-Knee Curl
Shoulder Release
Spinal Stretch

## DETAILED INSTRUCTIONS ON OFFICE ROUTINE TWO

### Neck Rolls
To relieve neck and shoulder tension, lift your shoulders up by your ears and rotate the neck and head in large circles three times in each direction. Relax the shoulders and repeat the rotations in each direction. If it bothers your neck to arch back, draw imaginary circles in front of you with your nose to achieve the neck rotation minus the tilting back of the neck.

Chest Expander

### Chest Expander
To release tension in the chest and shoulders, lean forward from your hips and clasp your hands together behind you. Continue to lean forward and inhale, both lifting your arms up behind you and lifting and opening your chest at the same time. Hold for three breaths. Lower your arms and take a complete breath. Repeat two more times.

### Upper Back and Shoulder Release
Place your feet on the carpet hip distance apart and clasp your hands over your head. Roll your palms toward the ceiling. Stretch through your elbows and gently stretch to one side, holding for one breath. Repeat to the other side. Practice again to each side.

Upper Back and Shoulder Release

## Elbow-to-Knee Curl

To trim the waist and strengthen the abdominal muscles, interlace your fingers behind your neck and lift the left knee. At the same time, bring the right elbow to the knee. Exhale as you lift the knee and elbow toward each other, and inhale as you lower the leg. Repeat to the other side. Practice the whole exercise four more times.

## Shoulder Release

To relax shoulder tension, bring your right arm up over your head and bend your elbow, placing your right hand on your upper back. Take your left hand and gently pull the right elbow behind your head. You can increase the stretch by pushing the back of your head against the right elbow and lifting your chest into correct posture. For a full stretch, bring your left hand to your upper back from below and clasp the fingers of both hands. Repeat to the other side. Do not do the full stretch if it is too much of a pull: Stay with gently pulling the elbow toward the back of your head.

Elbow-to-Knee Curl

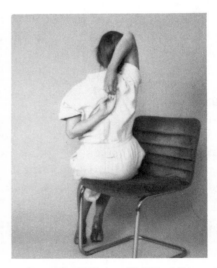

Shoulder Release

Shoulder Release (Full Stretch)

## Spinal Stretch

To stretch the spine and trim the waist, bend forward and place your right hand along your left leg or on your foot. Extend your left arm up toward the ceiling and look toward the extended left hand. Hold this position for three *Complete Breaths*. Repeat to the other side. If it feels like too much of a stretch for you, rather than placing your right hand on your foot, place your right forearm on your right thigh, and extend your left arm toward the ceiling. This is a gentle but effective side stretch and releases buildup of tension in the lower back. Repeat to the other side.

Spinal Stretch

# FINAL TIPS

## Correct Spinal Alignment

Throughout the day check your sitting posture. Sitting correctly and comfortably can slow down the buildup of tension. To protect your lower back, do not slouch back at the waist. As you sit at the telephone or at the computer, bend forward from the hips, not the waist. To prevent neck and shoulder strain, do not jut the neck forward. Look down with your eyes, not your neck! It helps to think of pushing back from the chin to keep the neck upright.

## Mental Breaks

Sit with your eyes closed and practice any of the deep relaxation, quiet time, or meditation exercises from this book for several minutes. This will give your eyes a rest and your mind a rest.

MUSCLES

# EXERCISES BY MUSCLE GROUP

SIT QUIETLY WITH YOUR EYES CLOSED and experience how your body feels. Notice where in your body you are holding tension. Next look at the figures on the following page, and note the number written in your area of tension. Use the *Exercises Listed by Muscle Group* listing to find the specific exercise that will release your physical stress.

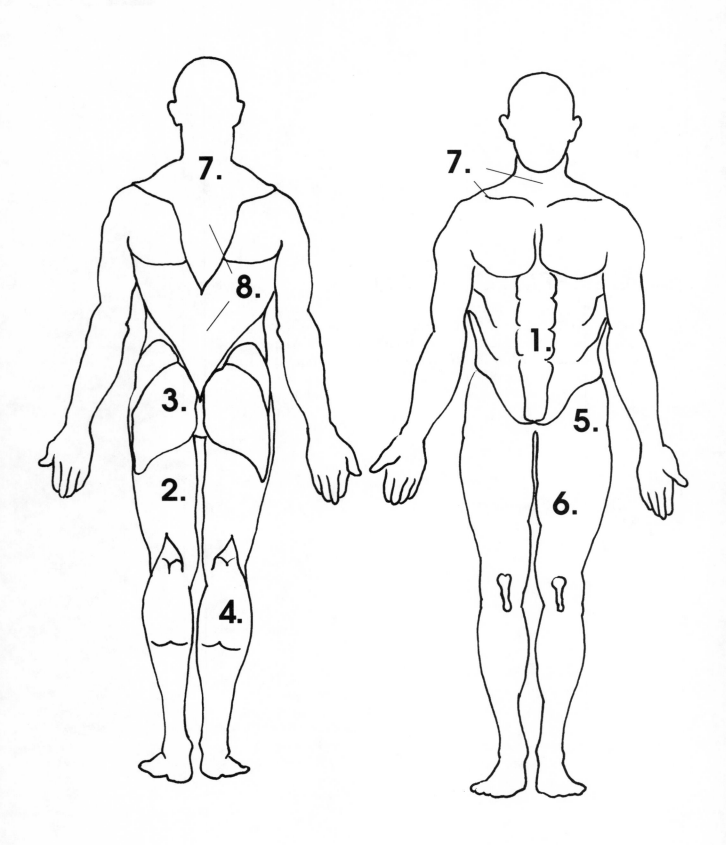

# EXERCISES LISTED BY MUSCLE GROUP

REFERENCES

1. Moser, M., M.D. *High Blood Presure and What You Can Do About It.* Elmsford, New York: The Benjamin Company, 1982.

2. Pelletier, K. R. *Mind as Healer Mind as Slayer.* New York: Dell Publishing Co., 1982.

3. Seyle, H. In Lynn Brallier. *Transition and Transformation: Successfully Managing Stress.* Los Altos, CA. National Nursing Review, 1982.

4. Way, D., M.D. *Anatomy and Physiology.* Unpublished Papers, Nevada City, CA. 1979.

5. Holmes, H. and Rahe, H. "The Social Readjustment Rating Scale." *Journal of Psychosomatic Research.* Vol. 11 pp. 213-218. New York: Pergamon Press, 1967.

6. Cousins, Norman. "A Nation of Hypochondriacs." *Time* Magazine. June 18, 1990; p. 88.

7. Benson, H. *The Relaxation Response.* New York: Avon Books, 1976.

8. Benson, H. *Beyond The Relaxation Response.* New York: Times Books, 1984.

9. O'Hara, Valerie. *Stress Management: A Holistic Approach.* Ph.D. Dissertation, San Diego: 1984.

10. In S. Bliss (ed.) *The New Holistic Health Handbook: Living Well In A New Age.* Lexington: Steven Green Press, 1985.

11. Jacobson, E. *Progressive Relaxation.* Chicago: University of Chicago Press, 1938.

12. Wathen, D. "Flexibility Roundtable." *NSCA Journal.* August-September, 1984; pp. 10-21.

13. Iyengar, B. K. S. *Light on Yoga.* New York: Schocker Books, 1979.

14. Kriyananda, S. *Yoga Postures for Higher Awareness.* Nevada City: Crystal Clarity Publications, 1985.

15. Shapiro, D. H. "Overview: Clinical and Physiological Comparison of Meditation with Other Self-Control Strategies." *American Journal of Psychiatry* 139, no. 3 (March 1982); p. 268.

16. Kriyananda, S. *The Fourteen Steps To Higher Awareness.* Nevada City: Crystal Clarity Publications, 1989.

17. Rama, S., Ballentine, R., and Ajaya, S. *Yoga and Psychotherapy: The Evolution of Consciousness.* Honesdale, PA: The Himalayan Institute, 1976.

18. Pelletier, K. R. *Mind as Healer Mind as Slayer.* New York: Dell Publishing Co., 1982; p. 224.

19. Smith, J. C. "Yoga and Stress." In S. Ajaya (ed.) *Meditational Therapy.* Glenview, Ill: The Himalayan Institute, 1977.

20. Carrington, P. *Freedom in Meditation.* Garden City, New York: Anchor Press, 1977.

21. Seyle, H. *The Stress of Life.* New York: McGraw hill, 1977.

22. Brallier, Lynn. Transition and Transformation: *Successfully Managing Stress.* Los Altos, CA: National Nursing Review, 1982.

23. Mason, J. L. *Guide to Stress Reduction.* Los Angeles: Citrus House Publishers, Inc., 1980.

24. Davis, M. *The Relaxation and Stress Reduction Workbook.* Oakland: New Harbinger Publications, 1982.

25. Bylinsky, G. "The New Assault on Heart Attacks." *Fortune* 113, no. 7 (March 31, 1986); pp. 80-89.

26. Bradshaw, John. *Healing The Shame That Binds You.* Deerfield Beach: Health Communications, Inc. 1988.

27. Borysenko, Joan *Minding The Body, Mending The Mind.* Reading: Addison Wesley, 1987.

28. Airola, P. *How To Get Well.* Phoenix: Health Plus Publishers, 1981: 269.

29. Diamond, H. and M. *Fit for Life.* New York: Warner Books, 1987.

30. Taub, Edward A. *Prescription for Life.* Sausalito: American Wellness Association, 1989.

31. Lappé, F. *Diet for A Small Planet Revisited.* New York: Ballantine Books, 1987; p. 181.

**INDEX**

# LA JOLLA INSTITUTE FOR STRESS MANAGEMENT

*offers the following*
*Fitness Option Program supplements:*

## Relaxations

Five 10-minute guided deep relaxations. Experience the most beneficial of all stress management techniques for release of physical and mental tension. Each 10-minute session of calming music—coupled with the soothing voice of Valerie O'Hara—leaves you feeling deeply relaxed and refreshed. **Audio Cassette: $11.00**

## Yoga with Valerie

A 60-minute video (VHS) of two, thirty-minute routines of breathing, stretching, yoga postures, and deep relaxation. One beginning and one intermediate routine. Beautiful garden and ocean settings. **Video Cassette: $35.00**

*Prices include tax, shipping, and handling.*
*Mail personal check to:*

**Valerie O'Hara**
**La Jolla Institute for Stress Management**
14618 Tyler Foote Road Suite 206
Nevada City, California 95959

*Visa/Master card accepted. Call toll-free 1-800-869-0581*